greater GLORY

LIVING YOUR LIFE
to THE GLORY of GOD

KRISTEN TIBER

Publishing and Design Services: MelindaMartin.me

ISBN: 978-0-9995876-1-4

www.KristenTiber.com

To all the women
who have and will join me
on this journey to
live for God's glory.

Soli Deo Gloria

Contents

Introduction.. 1

Week One   Show Me Your Glory.................................... 3

Week Two   Birthing an Ichabod 29

Week Three   Scattered Seed 55

Week Four   Fuel for the Fire 79

Week Five   Present Suffering 103

About the Author 128

How to Have a Personal Relationship with Jesus 129

Leader's Guide 132

Acknowledgements 134

Works Cited..135

Introduction

What do you live for? If you asked this question on the street, you would receive a wide variety of answers. I imagine the answers would be along the lines of: *I live for myself. I live for the job, for making money. I live for my kids and my family.* Some may answer with the cause currently on their heart or their desire to make the world a better place. I wonder how many would respond with "the glory of God" as their reason for existence. I wouldn't expect many. I am not even sure you'd find this answer to be prevalent in some churches after a Sunday morning service.

So what do *you* live for? Your answer to this question has the power to transform an ordinary life to extraordinary. And it all comes down to purpose. As I have prepared this study for you, I have been challenged myself to look at how I handle the big and small situations that arise in a typical existence on planet Earth. Will these experiences just begin and end with me? Or can they be used to bring God greater glory? The answer lies in the pages that follow.

My name is Kristen, and I am so glad you are here. We are about to start a great journey into the Word of God. We will be embarking on a topical study of God's glory and how our lives can serve to bring Him greater glory no matter our circumstance. I have been so very excited, albeit a bit intimidated, to cover what we are going to look at these next five weeks. Are you ready for some stretching, learning, growing and fun? I hope so! I know the Lord has great things in store for us.

We kick off this Bible study with a brief introduction video, which can be accessed at KristenTiber.com/GreaterGloryVideos. The workbook includes five weeks of study, with each week containing five lessons. There will be a video with me at the end of every week. All videos are accessible for free and found at the address above. These videos are an important part of our study; I hope you will be sure to watch them.

If you are working through this study with a group, you will find a Leader's Guide in the back of this workbook. When you see a question marked with a ✳, the answer to this question will be discussed during small group time. Don't worry if you can't answer every question.

I pray that through this study the Lord will reveal more of Himself to you, that you will grow deeper in your love for Jesus and discover how YOU can bring Him glory.

It's time to watch the Introduction Video, and then you'll be ready to start Week One!

For His Glory,

Week One
Show Me Your Glory

"LORD, I have heard of your fame;
I stand in awe of your deeds, LORD.
Repeat them in our day, in our time make them known;
in wrath remember mercy . . . .
His glory covered the heavens and his praise filled the earth.
His splendor was like the sunrise;
rays flashed from his hand,
where his power was hidden."

HABAKKUK 3:2-4

Before you begin this week, please watch the
Introduction Video accessible at
KristenTiber.com/GreaterGloryVideos.

Day One

Today, we begin a journey of discovery, growth, and faith. Oh how glad I am to be here with you! We will explore passages of Scripture that will light fires in our spirits and touch the most tender parts of our hearts. But we will also look at passages that will make us feel uncomfortable. We will face conviction, and at times, we may even struggle with understanding the ways God moves. But the big question is: will we keep going? Will we set our hearts to discover what glory is and how we can bring the Lord greater glory with our very own lives?

Write a prayer of commitment to God, asking for His help in seeing this study through.

One thing you will notice as we explore the concept of glory is that we, as followers of Christ, handle glory quite differently than others.

✤**When you think of our society's definition of glory, what comes to mind? Is it a biblical view of glory?**

✤**What do you think of when you consider glory from a biblical perspective?**

During our first week together, we will look at glory in the Bible. *What is it? How was it manifested? And what does it matter to us?*

The glory of God is a massive topic to look at in the Bible. I would like to sit here with you over a cup of coffee and tell you that the glory of God is a simple topic and *here* is the simple explanation. I would like to tell you that it is like a coin with two sides and can be looked at from *this* point of view or *that* point of view. But that is not the case.

The glory of God is more like what Thomas A. Rohm, a seminary professor of biblical languages, said when he compared God's glory to a multi-faceted diamond.[1] There are many faces, many aspects and when you look closely, you are only going to find that there is so much more to see!

Paul David Tripp captures the complexity of God's glory with this description of his visit to the Chicago Symphony Orchestra:

> *I will never forget that evening. I can't think of a moment when I was more blown away by a musical composition.*
>
> *I don't recall the composer or the conductor, but I was at a performance played by the Chicago Symphony Orchestra. My ticket put me in the first row and it was worth it. The music was powerful, foreboding, amazing, haunting, compelling, and glorious, all at the same time.*
>
> *There were moments when I wished this night would never end, and moments when I wanted to get up and run out of the concert hall. There were moments when the music caused my chest to rattle and moments when it lured me in with a whisper. There were moments when musical joy collided with musical fear in a beautiful disharmony of sound.*
>
> *When the performance was over, I felt both sad and exhausted. I wanted more, and yet at the same time I felt like I had had enough. I didn't know why this particular performance had affected me so deeply until I looked at the program and saw the name of the composition. It read:* **God, the most formidable word ever spoken.**[2]

He goes on to say, "For any human being to think that they could capture the glory of God in a single artistic statement is delusional at best and vain at worst."[3] And that is how we may feel when we think about His glory. There is no single statement to cover it all.

What we are going to do this first week is bring that jeweler's magnifier up to our eyes and look at the facets of the diamond. As we work through each of this week's lessons, we are going to trace the glory of God in a chronological way through the Bible. And what I hope is that when we are done, we will look at Him and say, "Wow!" and that we will have witnessed an exquisite glimpse of His glory. So, let's roll up our sleeves and get to work on understanding this concept of glory.

During the winter months in Ohio when the leaves are off of the trees, I am treated to some of the most amazing sunrises outside my bedroom window. There have been mornings when the sky looked ablaze with fiery colors of red and orange. On other mornings, soft pinks and blues melted into a gentle wakeup call to greet the day. When I witness such masterpieces, I cannot help but think of God's beauty, power and creativity. He is quite an artist!

This week, we will examine five ways in which God revealed His glory. At the end of Day One, you will find a chart. Please return to this chart throughout the week to fill in the boxes.

Describe a beautiful sunrise or sunset you have seen. Where were you?

Did the sight conjure up any feelings? How did it make you feel about God?

Let's look at what the Bible says about creation. Please turn to Genesis 1:1. What is the first verse in the Bible?

"In the beginning God created the _____ and the _____."

Please note: I will primarily be using the NIV throughout this study. But when a fill-in-the-blank is required, most versions will translate the passage with the same word.

Now, read Psalm 19:1. What does the psalmist tell us in the first part of this verse?

"The heavens declare the _____ of God."

Turn also to Psalm 97:6.

"The heavens proclaim his righteousness and all peoples see his _____."

Oh yes, the heavens declare the glory of God, and Psalm 19 goes on to say that the skies show the work of His hand. "They pour forth speech" (Psalm 19:2). When we look at creation, we can see God's glory! When we see natural revelation—that which He has made and revealed through nature—we see Him. God created this world to point to His glory.[4]

In the first box on Tracing the Glory on page 9, write the word: *creation*.

One thing you may not know about me is that I am a Disney World junkie. I love the Disney parks! The fun, creativity, imagination, attention to detail . . . it just gets me every time. My husband can make it about five days and then is ready to hop on a plane home. Me? I could stay well beyond what my wallet can afford. And the moment we get home, I begin dreaming about going back. Consider this illustration from Paul David Tripp.

> *Imagine taking a family vacation to Disney World, and 30 miles out, you spot a sign on the side of the road with the logo and name of the resort. It would be silly to stop at the sign and have your family vacation on the side of the road! So it is with the glory of God in creation—it's only a sign, directing you to the source. Don't stop at the sign.*[5]

God created this world to point to His glory.

When we look around at the magnificence and the breadth of His creation, the variety of His creativity—the spectacular mountains, the quiet rivers, and the beautiful flowers—we can see His glory in the essence and value of what He has made. This is natural revelation. Creation was the first way that man was able to see the bigger picture of God's glory far beyond the creativity and imagination of any theme park.

What do you specifically notice in nature that points to God's glory?

Why do you think some miss the connection between creation and His glory?

How can you better appreciate the wonderful masterpiece of God's creation?

Lord, help us to see Your glory in the world You created—from the most delicate of butterflies and sweetest of flowers to the roar of the mighty lion and the great expanse of a fiery sunrise.

As you go about your day today, try to focus on the ways God has made Himself known through creation. Tomorrow, we will see the next way God revealed His glory . . . and it is going to be good!

End today by praising God for the beauty and wonders of His creation.

Tracing the Glory

```
┌─────────────────────────────┐
│                             │
│                             │
└─────────────────────────────┘
              │
┌─────────────────────────────┐
│                             │
│                             │
└─────────────────────────────┘
              │
┌─────────────────────────────┐
│                             │
│                             │
└─────────────────────────────┘
              │
┌─────────────────────────────┐
│              /              │
│                             │
└─────────────────────────────┘
              │
┌─────────────────────────────┐
│                             │
│                             │
└─────────────────────────────┘
```

Day Two

Today, we are going to let our fingers walk us through portions of Exodus as we continue to track God's glory through the Bible. We will take a look at some of the moments when the Lord showed His glory and manifested His presence in a visible and physical way. Together, let's catch a glimpse of what Moses and the Israelites saw so many years ago in the desert.

Allow me to give you a little context for our first passage. The Israelites had just left the bondage of the Egyptians. Following the tenth and final plague (the death of all of Egypt's firstborn), Pharaoh told the Israelites to leave, and God led them out into the desert toward the Red Sea.

And how did He lead? Let's take a look.

Read Exodus 13:20-22.

The Lord led the Israelites with the pillar of _____ and the pillar of _____.

Here we see the pillar of cloud and the pillar of fire. This is what Jewish Rabbis called the *Shekinah* (shuh KIGH nuh) glory of God. Maybe you've heard this term before. The Shekinah glory was a physical and visible manifestation of God's glory on earth. This is your next response on our chart, Tracing the Glory, found on page 9: *Shekinah*.

Now, the word "Shekinah" doesn't actually appear in the Bible. But this is what the physical, manifested presence of God was called by Rabbis before the time of the New Testament and by biblical scholars of today. The word means "dwelling" or "one who dwells," [6] and that is important to remember for later in our study.

> The Shekinah glory was a physical and visible manifestation of God's glory on earth.

Over the next couple of days, I would like you to note a few things about the Shekinah glory. First, the Shekinah glory refers to the divine presence of God. Now, could God be present without the Shekinah? Absolutely! But know that where the Shekinah glory was, it was unmistakable that God was present there.

For those of you with older kids, you may remember arriving at the point in raising your children when they were old enough to shower by themselves. But for some children, you questioned the quality of their—*how do I put this delicately?*—hygiene. You know, how well they actually washed themselves and how thoroughly they scrubbed their head. Many years ago, we were in this stage with my son, Peter. I did not think that kid was washing his hair well enough, so we worked out a system. He would wash his body, then knock on the wall, and I would know he was ready for me to come lather up and scrub his head.

Well, on one particular morning, I was putting on my makeup and had just completed applying mascara to one of my eyes when the knock came. I thought this could be rather funny to see if Peter noticed the fact that one eye had mascara and one did not. And you should know that there is a BIG difference between my eyelashes having mascara on them and when they do not. I thought this could be pretty amusing to see if he noticed. Of course he would notice, right?

I went into the kids' bathroom and reached in to wash his hair and he was looking right at me. I asked him, "Peter, do you notice anything different about me?"

He looked and responded, "No."

So I said, "Peter, look at my face."

He took a few seconds and repeated plainly, "No."

Being somewhat exasperated, I instructed, "PETER, *look at my eyes.*"

And he took a couple of seconds and looked carefully. He cocked his head a little. He paused and then replied, "You mean the bags under your eyes?"

Here what I thought was unmistakably obvious was not at all obvious to him. Well, let me tell you: When the Shekinah glory shows up, there is no mistaking it. It is obvious that the divine presence of God is there and it is visible!

> The Shekinah glory refers to the divine presence of God.

Has God made Himself unmistakably present to you at different times in your life? In what ways?

Examples of the Shekinah glory are peppered throughout the Old Testament such as Moses' burning bush, the pillar of cloud, and the pillar of fire, and we will see others as well. God's glory in these cases is physical, visible, and of divine nature.

Turn to Exodus 14:19-20. When the Israelites were running from the Egyptians, what moved behind the people to block the armies of Egypt?

Can you imagine being an Israelite at this time leaving Egypt? The Israelites were in slavery for 430 years. Yes, they knew the stories of Abraham, Isaac, and Jacob, but their world had shrunk to brick-making and horrendous conditions of manual labor under their Egyptian oppressors. What would they have thought as they watched the plagues strike the Egyptians but not their fellow Hebrews? What was going through their minds as the pillar of cloud moved ahead and behind them, or when the seas parted and they were able to walk across on dry ground? Their God was showing up big on their behalf!

"Who among the gods is like you, LORD? Who is like you— majestic in holiness, awesome in glory, working wonders?"

—EXODUS 15:11

I love the part of Moses' song following the crossing of the Red Sea in Exodus 15:11 when he asked, "Who is like you . . . ?" (You can read the entire verse in the margin.) Who *is* like our God? There is none! When you think of all He is, all He does—who is like Him? There is none!

✢ **What amazes you about our God?**

✢ **Read Psalm 89:8. What question does the psalmist ask and what characteristics does he note about the Lord?**

In Psalm 35:10, David shares, "My whole being will exclaim, 'Who is like you, LORD?'"

When you think about it, it is pretty awesome that unlike any other religion, any other faith, this God, the God of the entire universe, calls us to seek His face and to have a relationship with Him. He doesn't call us to worship from afar and serve Him like robots in our devotion to Him. No, He calls us to seek His face and to know Him as friend. Whoa! *Who is like Him??* I don't know about you, but I find that pretty exciting!

Day Three

I can remember times when my kids were very young, and they would become ravenously hungry. It wasn't "Mommy, I am hungry. Could we please stop and get something to eat?" It was anguish and melt downs as their little bodies couldn't sustain any longer without nourishment.

As we continue to look at the Shekinah glory, let's start in Exodus 16 when Aaron (Moses' brother) addresses the Hebrew crowd. The Israelites had left Egypt and were complaining of hunger . . . even to the point of thinking it would have been better to have died in bondage in Egypt. That is some serious hangry attitude going on! But the Lord is compassionate and patient, and He tells Moses that He will send manna in the morning and meat in the evening.

> **Read Exodus 16:9-12. Imagine you are an Israelite standing among the people while Aaron spoke.**

> **What appeared in the cloud?** _____

> **What do we call this?** _____ **glory.**

If you were an Israelite, what would you have thought seeing the Shekinah glory?

What was God's purpose of the quail, manna and cloud of glory (verse 12)?

Let's allow our fingers to lead us through more of Exodus. As we flip through the pages of this book, we're going to pass the water coming from the rock and the defeat of the Amalekites where Moses had to continuously keep his arms raised in order to be victorious (Exodus 17). We're going to walk to Mount Sinai (Exodus 19) where the Israelites again witnessed manifestations of His presence—the thick cloud hovering over the mountain and the Lord descending in fire. Turn now to Exodus 24.

Read Exodus 24:15-18 and watch for the Shekinah glory. Who entered the cloud? _____

Exodus 24 is the chapter where the covenant is confirmed, and then God spends the next seven chapters giving instructions for the building of the tabernacle. The tabernacle was to be a transitory type of temple, where sacrifices would be offered and where the Shekinah glory would dwell in the Holy of Holies.

When you look in the Old Testament, there are many Hebrew words for *glory*, but the most commonly used is *kabowd* (kaw-bode'). I discovered it written both as *kabowd* or with more Jewish commentators, *kavod*. This word appears 200 times in the Old Testament and is the word for glory in all the passages at which we have looked.

This word *kabowd* (glory) is incredibly interesting because of what it means and signifies. The Hebrew word means "weight, splendor and copiousness."[7] Now, what in the world does weight have to do with God's glory? Splendor, we can grasp. Copiousness—abundant in supply and quantity, meaning God has plenty to go around—is something to which we can relate. *But weight?*

Why do you think weight might have something to do with God's glory?

Glory is something that is heavy, magnificent—so incredible both in manifestation and concept. If you are old enough, you may remember some of the movies from the 80s when someone would share something big or mind-blowing, the response was, "Whoa, heavy." That's this. Glory is heavy. Tommy Tenney describes God's glory as "His weighty presence."[8]

And that is the second thing I would like you to know about the Shekinah glory. The Hebrew word for glory, kabowd, draws our attention to the weight of His presence.

I have to tell you, there were days when I was researching for this Bible study that I felt so heavy looking at all this because—whoa—there is nothing light and easy about studying the glory of the King. It *is* heavy!

When I taught this study to a group of ladies at my church, I wished I could have walked in with a ton of bricks simply to give the the visual representation of the weight of His glory. It can be our tendency to think of a cloud as light and pretty. Poof. It moves and is gone. But no, this is a cloud with the weight of bricks! His presence is weighty and something with which not to be trifled. *Hard Sayings of the Bible* notes, "The glory of God refers first and foremost to the sheer weight of his presence."[9]

I like the way Professor Rohm defined glory:

> *Glory is the manifested presence of God, often displayed in dazzling magnificence; it is His character, His attributes expressed; it is His weight, His inestimable worth revealed in His creation.*[10]

The Hebrew word for glory, kabowd, draws our attention to the weight of His presence.

What are your thoughts on glory after reading this definition?

Have you ever felt the weight of His presence? In what way(s)?

Here in Exodus 24, Moses walked into the cloud and stayed for forty days and nights. After receiving the instructions for building and equipping the tabernacle, Moses returned from the mountain and found Aaron and the people had created something to worship.

Read Exodus 32:1-6. What did the people make out of gold?

____

- **If you think about it, everyone worships something. What kinds of things does our culture worship?**

- **Is it easy for Christians to become caught up with these things? Why or why not?**

- **When you compare those things to the greatness of God and the weight of His glory, why do you think we keep choosing those other things?**

**Do idols take up any space in your life? How can you
dethrone them?**

After everything God had done for the Israelites, Moses found the people danc-
ing around a golden calf and worshipping it. His response? His anger burned.
And without any disrespect to Moses, I have to tell you that I find it humorously
ironic what Moses did next and how he handled disciplining the Israelites for
the choices they made.

We see in verses 19-20 that Moses first took the golden calf and burned it in the
fire. Then, he ground it into powder and scattered it in the water. And as if to
reserve the most epic action for last, he then made the Israelites drink it.

I am listening to an audio book on raising life-ready kids—it's a great book.[11]
The approach is for parents to talk less and establish natural (when possible) and
intentional consequences for wrong-doing and disobedience. Parents shouldn't
rescue their kids as is the tendency for many of us. If something happens, a
parent should let it play out. Consequences follow all our actions even into
adulthood and the point is to learn the lesson when young.

When I see Moses carrying through with this extensive consequence, I can't help
but see the actions of a deliberate parent, talking less and letting the consequence speak for itself. "Hey, you want to worship this? Well, you better be
ready to drink it all the way down." And Moses actually made the idolatrous
Israelites drink the burned, ground up and water-logged memory of their once
worshipped calf. Oh dear! If I did this, my kids would be completely freaked out
and possibly forever scarred. But I can guarantee one thing: it would be a lesson
never forgotten.

Because of this idolatry, Moses made atonement for the (now repentant) people,
and God tells Moses that He will still give them the land, but He will not go
with them. We will talk about this in our end-of-the week video. Watch the
video before starting week two on your own or with your group. Don't miss it!
It's going to be Moses-level intense.

See you tomorrow as we continue to follow the glory.

Day Four

Not too long ago, a friend of mine was in a car accident. She and her husband were returning from a long road trip and less than ten minutes from home. They stopped on the road, waiting for the car in front of them to turn left. But from behind, they were struck by a teenage girl not paying attention. Because of the speed at which they were hit, my friend's car lunged forward, striking the car in front of them as well. The 3-car accident was enough to make anyone upset and angry.

But instead of yelling at the driver or becoming bitter, what did my friend do? She stood there with her arm around the teen girl's shoulders comforting her. The young driver was sobbing and apologetic. And there was my friend exhibiting Jesus' love and compassion to a stranger. My friend's response to the situation revealed what was in her heart. And more and more, I am realizing that the way in which we respond to a situation really does divulge what is in our hearts. Do you agree?

Open your Bible and read Exodus 33:7-11. I would like you to pay particular attention to the response of the people in this passage.

When Moses went out to the tent, what did the people do?

And then when the pillar of cloud, the Shekinah glory, came down (verse 10), how did the people respond?

What does this behavior signify?

With what attitude do we approach the Lord? Keep something here in Exodus 33, and let's quickly look at Ezekiel 1. I would like you to see Ezekiel's response when he sees the glory of God in a vision.

Read Ezekiel 1:25-28. Describe the one like a man who Ezekiel saw.

✣ **In verse 28, what did Ezekiel do?**

"So I got up and went to the plain. And the glory of the LORD was standing there, like the glory I had seen by the Kebar River, and I fell facedown."

—EZEKIEL 3:23

In Ezekiel 3:12, the Spirit lifts up Ezekiel, and he hears a loud rumbling sound as the glory of the LORD rises from the place where it was standing. Look in 3:23. Again, what did Ezekiel do in response?

✣ **Why did Ezekiel do this?**

When we experience God's glory, our response will always be one of respect, humility, and worship.

When we feel or experience the weight of His glory, what else are we going to do but fall facedown? For real! I often think, the *more* we see of Him, the *more* we are going to be spending time on our faces.

The Israelites stood at their tents and worshipped. Ezekiel fell facedown. And in Leviticus 9:24, I'll just tell you that as the priests were beginning their ministry and the glory appeared, the people shouted for joy . . . and *then* fell facedown. When we experience God's glory, our response will always be one of respect, humility, and worship.

❖ **Is this what is in your heart? Are you where you need to be in your response to God? Why or why not?**

Turn now to Exodus 40. The tabernacle has been built. This was to be God's dwelling place, a pre-temple version which could move with the people. Look in verses 34-38, and let's get a sneak peek of what happens at the dedication of the tabernacle.

What filled the tabernacle? _____

Yes, the Shekinah glory of God. It filled the tabernacle, and there, God dwelled with His people. Fast forward about 500 years,[12] and God called David's son, Solomon, to build the stationary temple in Jerusalem, which God also occupied with the physical and visible Shekinah glory.

Read 2 Chronicles 7:1-3. (Read through verse 10 for extra enjoyment.) What came down from heaven and consumed the burnt offering?

Why could the priests not enter the temple?

How did the Israelites respond?

While the glory filled this temple built by Solomon, once it was destroyed by Nebuchadnezzar in 586 BC, the Shekinah glory never returned to the temple rebuilt by Zerubbabel or to Herod's temple. The appearance of the temple glory concluded with Nebuchadnezzar's destruction of the temple, at which time many Jews were exiled to Babylon.

Ezekiel, in a vision in Ezekiel 10, spoke about seeing the glory depart from the temple. Can you imagine seeing the glory leave the temple? The divine presence of God simply going away, out the east gate? For the Israelite, I can't imagine the grief of that image. In later years however, Haggai shared of a new glory. One beyond comparison to this temple glory. The Lord said in Haggai 2:9, "The glory of this present house [the one that is coming] will be greater than the glory of the former house. And in this place I will grant peace."

Despite the glory departing, the Israelites would have known that Ezekiel also foresaw God's glory returning to the temple (Ezekiel 43). Therefore, they would have held out hope. Hope that would years later be fulfilled as a multitude of angels filled the sky, and the glory of God appeared before a band of shepherds.

And nearly 600 years after Ezekiel's vision, the glory does return to the temple.

"the image of the invisible God"

—COLOSSIANS 1:15

Turn to Luke 2. Let's read verses 22-32.

"the Lord of glory"

—HEBREWS 1:3

Why did Mary and Joseph take Jesus to Jerusalem?

"the radiance of God's glory"

—1 CORINTHIANS 2:8

This Jesus—of whom Scripture calls "the image of the invisible God," "the Lord of glory," and "the radiance of God's glory" (Colossians 1:15, Hebrews 1:3, 1 Corinthians 2:8)—this Jesus enters Jerusalem as a 40-day old baby for purification rites. Two young, Jewish parents bring this little child to present Him to the Lord according to the law. And when they step across the threshold, the glory of God re-enters the temple.

Imagine with me the excitement in the heavenlies right before this moment—the anticipation of the glory, the Messiah, with his parents stepping foot into the temple. I just get chills. Don't you wish we could see on that heavenly realm—the flurry, the buzz, and the elation? How I would have loved to see the precious glory of God wrapped in a little baby in a blanket crossing the threshold and the glory ushered back into the temple.

Look at John 1:14. "The Word became flesh and made his _____ among us."

> Jesus is the manifested glory of God in human form with a covering of flesh, dwelling among us.

That word "dwelling" means "tabernacled." Think back to the glory filling the tabernacle but here, the Lord put on flesh and walked among us. Continuing in John 1:14, "We have seen his glory, the glory of the one and only Son . . . ." Do you remember back to the meaning of Shekinah? It means "dwelling or one who dwells." Jesus made His dwelling among us. Jesus is the manifested glory of God in human form with a covering of flesh, dwelling among us. That's incredible! Turn back to our Tracing the Glory chart on page 9 and fill in His name in the third box: *Jesus.*

And what did Jesus bring? According to Haggai, the glory of the new house would bring peace. Peace with God. Salvation and forgiveness of sin through His death on a cross in our place brings lasting peace with God. We, who were once enemies (Romans 5:10, Colossians 1:21-22), are now called daughters of the Most High (John 1:12, 1 John 3:1).

We are not going to turn to this next passage, but the transfiguration of Christ is too awesome not to at least mention. In Luke 9:28-36, Jesus, Peter, James, and John went to the mountain to pray and Jesus' appearance began to change. It became as bright as a flash of lightning. Moses and Elijah appeared in glorious splendor. The glory of God appeared, and the cloud covered them. Then God spoke and said, "This is my Son, in whom I am well pleased." Here we see Jesus in His glory, the Shekinah glory *and* the Father's pleasure and delight in His Son. Wow!

Furthermore, in 2 Corinthians 4:6, we read that the glory of God is displayed in the face of Christ. All that glory, embodied in Jesus and revealed in His face.

Are you as in awe as I am? The God we serve is mighty and powerful . . . and just downright cool! As we look at the face of Jesus, let's be sure our heartfelt response to His glory is appropriate. I am about to get my face in the carpet. Care to join me?

Take a moment and journal your thoughts:

If you would like to read more about salvation and having a personal relationship with Jesus, please turn to page 129.

Day Five

Can you imagine being on the mount of transfiguration with Jesus and with Peter, James and John? The sight would have been glorious! But what would surpass even that moment, would later be seeing the resurrected Jesus appear before their very eyes. Think about it. Three years spent with their beloved teacher only to be brought to an abrupt end with a horrific death on a cross. The devasting blow would have sent the followers into disarray. But then, glory! How absolutely amazing it would have been to see their resurrected Lord alive and well! I am so thankful we serve a living God, aren't you?

The resurrection is not only evidence that we serve a living God, but it also shows us that Jesus' sacrifice on the cross on our behalf was accepted by God the Father. Our position before God is now restored, and we can be at peace with God.

Well, where do we go from here? What aspect of glory is there left to trace? We still have two more stops, and we will cover both of them today. As we wind down the road of this journey, I am reminded of driving on the mountain roads of West Virginia when I was a teenager with my mom, my brother, and my friend. Our minivan was filled to the brim with belongings. Our bikes were craftily tied to the roof. We were ready for a fun week in sunny South Carolina. As we zoomed along, our car started to have trouble getting up the hills of the

Appalachian Mountains. Chugging is never a good sign on a road trip, especially when you're only halfway to your destination. Quite unexpectedly, we soon found ourselves on a three-hour hiatus at a mountain top McDonalds. But there we were with all our belongings unpacked in the parking lot, waiting for a tow truck to take the van for repairs and for a rental car to arrive so we could continue on our way. It was not what we expected on our journey.

Likewise, this next stop of glory may come as a bit of a surprise because it is *you*. You are the next stop as we trace the glory through history. Believe it or not, you are tied to the glory of God as a believer in Jesus.

> **Read 2 Corinthians 3:18. Into whose glorious image are we now being transformed?** _____

> **Insert your name into the following statement and then take a moment to consider the thought:**

> **Now, the work of His glory is seen in** _____ **.**

You see, God's greatest work now is in the human heart. You are the work of His glory. (Write your name in the first half of the fourth box on our Tracing the Glory chart, page 9.)

> **Look at Ephesians 3:14-21. Please pay particular attention to how often Paul used "you" or "your" in the text. List below those things for which Paul desired and asked of the Father.**

Did you notice the kind of riches Paul mentioned in verse 16? I like the way the *King James Version* phrased this: "That he would grant you, according to the riches of his glory, to be strengthened with might by his Spirit in the inner man." The riches of His glory!

Look again at verse 17. Where might Christ dwell?

Remember with me that the word Shekinah means "one who dwells or dwelling."[13] Christ dwells. He tabernacles. But where? In *your* heart through faith. God's divine presence dwells in your heart. Christ in you, the hope of glory (Colossians 1:27).

In verse 19, what is to fill us to the measure?

We are to be filled to the measure with the fullness of God—all that He is, His essence. No other religion has the indwelling of the deity in the follower. Christianity is different because we have Christ and in us, His Spirit has taken up residence. His dwelling within us and His power at work in us is to bring Him glory. What we do now, the way we renew our minds, the way we use our words, the way we act as believers can all bring Him glory.

Now catch the end of Ephesians 3. Take notice of where else we read that the glory is manifested? Read verse 21 again and fill in the blank. ". . . to him be glory in the _____ and in Christ Jesus throughout all generations, for ever and ever! Amen."

The glory is also to reside in the church. Looking at our chart on page 9, the second half of the fourth box is *church*. His glory is to show up in the body of believers. We are to be marked by His presence.

I remember in college, we had to learn the beginning of the Westminster Catechism. It was so simple and yet, so profound. "What is the chief end of man? Man's chief end is to glorify God, and enjoy Him forever." I love that. Glorify God and enjoy Him forever.

�֍ **How can YOU glorify God?**

�֍ **What does it mean to enjoy Him forever?**

Now, we have one last stop in tracing the glory and that is the future glory—the glory still on the horizon.

> **Turn to Revelation 21:9-27 and enjoy reading about our future glory. Afterward, you may fill in the final box on our Tracing the Glory chart on page 9 as *future glory* or *Heaven*.**

> **What provides the light in the new Jerusalem?**

We look forward to a future glory where we will see Him as He is, where nothing will be obscured. And according to Revelation 21:23, neither the sun nor the moon will be needed because God's glory itself gives it light.

John Piper put it this way, "Heaven will be a never-ending, ever-increasing discovery of more and more of God's glory with greater and ever-greater joy in Him."[14]

We can know we have a magnificent future glory to which we look forward. Truly, heaven will be something more than we can ever think or imagine. Praise Him! I look forward to that day when we will be completely and beautifully surrounded by His glory. How incredible it will be!

And while we wait in expectation of that glorious day, we can bring Him glory—right here and now. We can live lives worthy of being called His children. We seek to bring glory to the Father as we invite Him to freely dwell and reign in our hearts, being filled to the measure all for His glory!

> "Heaven will be a never-ending, ever-increasing discovery of more and more of God's glory with greater and ever-greater joy in Him."
> —John Piper

If you haven't yet watched the Introduction Video, please do so now. I share a personal story that became the reason behind this study. Visit KristenTiber.com/GreaterGloryVideos.

Want some extra reading?

Check out the glory of the new covenant in 2 Corinthians 3:7-18.

Show Me Your Glory

One of our greatest _____ in life can be that we are _____ by God.

Our _____ _____ should be to know God better and to long for His presence in our lives.

The glory of God, His divine presence, was the _____ _____ on the people of God.

God's glory encompasses all that He is; His very _____.

"But Moses would not be able to endure the spectacular purity, luminosity and reality of staring at the raw glory of God himself. Instead, God would protect Moses from accidental (and apparently fatal) sight of that glory . . . Only after his glory, or presence, had passed by would God remove his gracious, protecting 'hand.' . . . Moses did not see the glory of God directly, but once it had gone past, God did allow him to view the results, the afterglow, that his presence had produced."[15]

Upon witnessing God's glory, Moses assumes the proper position of _____ and he _____.

Video lessons are available at KristenTiber.com/GreaterGloryVideos.

Week Two
Birthing an Ichabod

"This is to my Father's glory, that you bear much fruit,
showing yourselves to be my disciples.
As the Father has loved me, so have I loved you.
Now remain in my love. If you keep my commands,
you will remain in my love,
just as I have kept my Father's commands
and remain in his love.
I have told you this so that my joy may be in you
and your joy may be complete."

JOHN 15:8-11

Day One

Welcome back! Last week, we traced the glory of God through the Scriptures. We saw God's glory revealed through creation, through the Shekinah glory, through Jesus, through us, as believers, and then finally, in the future glory. It was like seeing snapshots of each instance. And if last week was flipping through the photo album of those pictures, these next several weeks will be pulling out a magnifying glass so we can look nice and close at *our part* of the album. We will focus on our place in relationship to God's glory and how *we* can bring Him greater glory.

The next three weeks of Bible study find their foundation in one of my favorite Scripture verses: Isaiah 26:8. "Yes, LORD, walking in the way of your laws, we wait for you; your name and renown are the desire of our hearts."

Think about what this verse means. Rewrite it in your own words.

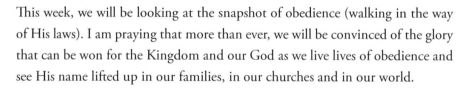

This week, we will be looking at the snapshot of obedience (walking in the way of His laws). I am praying that more than ever, we will be convinced of the glory that can be won for the Kingdom and our God as we live lives of obedience and see His name lifted up in our families, in our churches and in our world.

But what I have found to be tricky here is that obedience is one of those subjects that is so often avoided. No one really likes it. It's like those pictures of ex-boyfriends or ex-girlfriends that you just want to tear apart and throw out. Or you can be like my mother-in-law and literally cut the heads of her kids' former boyfriends and girlfriends out of the photos, leaving the rest of the image intact. After Dan's parents went on to be with the Lord, all the kids and their spouses went through containers of old photographs, and we had a good laugh over how often we came across a photo with a hole cut into it.

✤ **Why do you think obedience is a taboo subject in our society? Why does our culture fight the idea of obedience?**

Even though our culture may not like it, for the believer, obedience is part of the Christian life. I was listening to Chip Ingram the other day, and he shared what his professor, Howard Hendricks, told the class. The well-known teacher advised that God will never love us more than He does today. But His blessing is based on our obedience.[16]

✤ **What do you think this means? Do you agree or disagree?**

His blessing is based on your obedience. And I am going to add that the glory you bring the Father, therefore, is also tied very much to the level of obedience you exhibit in your life as others watch on.

✤ **How do you personally feel about obedience?**

This week, we're going to spend some time working through 1 Samuel 4. But today, let's back up a few verses and get the lay of the land with a little context.

Please read 1 Samuel 3:19-21. Where did the Lord continue to appear? _____

What was special about Shiloh? What are we talking about here? Turn to Joshua 18:1. What did the Israelites set up in Shiloh?

_____

If your Bible translation uses "tent of meeting," know that this tent of meeting wasn't the little tent Moses used in Exodus 33. This was the full-scale tabernacle—the mobile place of worship for which God gave Moses detailed building instructions when Moses was up on the mountain. This was *that* tabernacle.

And what do we know would appear in the tabernacle? (Look back at Exodus 40:34-38 if you need a refresher.)

So, the glory of God was in the tabernacle. And the tabernacle was in Shiloh. We need to know this as we jump into our passage this week.

Shiloh was the first major worship site for the Jews before the building of the temple in Jerusalem. It was a place of worship and where the annual sacrifices were made to the Lord. The tabernacle resided in Shiloh from the time of Joshua and during the period of the judges to the point we come to today in 1 Samuel. In Jeremiah 7:12, God called Shiloh the place where He first made a dwelling for His name. There is that word again, "dwelling."

Where have we seen the word "dwelling" before?

Now within the curtains of the tabernacle, where did God's glory dwell specifically? In the innermost part of the tabernacle was the ark of the covenant—also called the ark of the testimony.

Read Exodus 25:22. Where did God say He would meet with the people?

Look at Leviticus 16:2. Where did the cloud appear?

This ark of the covenant was a box of acacia wood, covered with pure gold. Two cherubim were on the lid, and between them formed a seat, called the mercy seat (or atonement cover). It was here that the blood was sprinkled once a year by the high priest for the atonement of sin. And it was also here that the Shekinah glory rested.

Now, just for fun: What was kept in the ark? See Hebrews 9:4 for help.

And that is what sets us up for our story. We are off to a good start! See you here tomorrow.

What did you learn about Shiloh today?

Day Two

With the importance of the glory, the ark, and Shiloh in mind, let's now start our journey in 1 Samuel 4.

Read 1 Samuel 4:1. Who were the Israelites fighting against?

We don't have to go any further than verse one to see an initial act of disobedience on the part of the Israelites. And it is simply this: they were not commanded to go fight the Philistines. God was the one to tell them when to go to battle and how to go to battle. But this fight, they took upon themselves. They did not seek God on how to handle the situation and how to overcome the oppression of the Philistines. Instead, they decided to go to war on their own. And the result will confirm the self-guided endeavor was wrong.

War is a pretty big thing to embark upon without the direction and authority of the Most High. Before we hurry off to do something big in our own lives, we would be wise to make sure God is with us.

Have you ever rushed into a decision without consulting God or determining His will? What was the result?

If we want God's best for our lives, it will always be found in a life of obedience and submitting to His authority. Whether it is related to job, family, finances, or school—whatever it may be—coming under His authority will mean seeking His will for direction and then following it. Sometimes, a quick evaluation of the situation will make it clear which direction to take based on what God has revealed in His Word. But at other times, we may find ourselves in a position of needing to take the time to find out what the Lord wants so we can follow Him.

This is not what the Israelites did.

After Dan and I had been married for a year, he was approached with a new job opportunity. He had been with his employer for ten years and loved it there. His co-workers had become family, and he is not one to be excited about big change. However, the person who reached out to him had been a previous boss and was a man who Dan really admired, respected, and trusted. He agreed to meet out of politeness with this man, but really, he had no desire to change jobs.

When that meeting led to phone conversations and dinners to meet other employees at the company, Dan began to feel quite torn. He saw the pros and cons with both choices (staying at old company/changing to the new one). It was such a big decision. He didn't know what to do. However, the one thing he could do was seek God and trust that the Lord would provide the right direction. And while his heart was certainly conflicted at times, he trusted the One who saw the big picture and loved him.

For weeks, we longed for an answer. *And it took weeks.* Our repeated and desperate prayer for direction became based on Psalm 40:8, "I desire to do your will . . . ." So we prayed:

> Lord, we don't know what is best. You do, and we desire to do Your will. Lord, You know the future You have for us. We desire to do Your will. Lord, guide us as You see fit because all we want is to follow You and do Your will.

Eventually, the Lord answered. The direction was to move forward with the new job, and Dan obeyed. And while the last fifteen years at this job haven't always been easy, we have clearly seen over and over again that it was God's best for Dan for this season. Glory to God!

If we want God's best for our lives and a life that will be most impactful to those around us, it means obedience and submission to His authority. Now in our disobedience, can the Lord use our mistakes? Yes! Absolutely. But that is no *excuse* for disobedience.

"I desire to do your will, my God; your law is within my heart."

—PSALM 40:8

If we want God's best for our lives, it will always be found in a life of obedience and submitting to His authority.

Read what Paul says about grace in Romans 6:1-2. Are we to continue sinning so that grace may increase? _____

We should not willingly disobey, thinking He will make good out of it somehow and thereby excuse our sin. That's just crazy. You'll never know the blessings that could have been. The Israelites in 1 Samuel 4 had forgotten that God's best always comes with obedience.

Are you ready to submit to God's authority in your life, or are you still fighting against obedience?

Before we read the next verse, I would like you to notice that the Bible gives us the locations of each army camp. Don't let anyone ever tell you that the Bible is just a collection of stories, myths, and legends. The Bible shares over 25,000 specific places in the Old Testament alone that can be verified in history.[17] Isn't that cool?

Back to 1 Samuel. The Israelites went to battle without seeking direction from God, and look at what transpired in verse 2.

Read 1 Samuel 4:2. What happened?

Defeat came. Every time God had ever commanded the people of Israel to go to battle, did they ultimately win or lose? They won. (For examples, see Joshua 5:13-6:27, Joshua 9, and 1 Samuel 23:1-5.) Every time they obeyed, it brought victory. Here, they went out without God's direction, and they faced defeat. They lost about 4,000 men on the battlefield!

I am wondering if there is anyone reading this text who has gone and done something that wasn't in God's will, and it wasn't until after she was bloody and bruised from battle that she realized she was never supposed to be there in the first place. The people of Israel were not walking in God's favor because they were not walking in the way of His laws. Whether we are on the battlefield or we are *making* our life a battlefield, when we disobey God's authority in our lives, we need to get ready for some rough roads ahead. He will allow those times of difficulty, struggle, and hardship in order to bring us back to Him.

We cannot expect success or long-term victory in anything we do if we are not following the laws and precepts of God. If we want success in our business, we can't be lying and cheating on our taxes. If we want strong, godly friendships, we can't be talking behind our friends' backs. If we want success in our marriage, we can't be flirting with other relationships. One example that comes to mind is living together before marriage. All couples can struggle at times in their marriage, but so often Dan and I have noticed an unusual increase of conflict when the couple lived together before saying, "I do." Why? Because by living together, the couple chose to go outside the precepts of God's design and plan. Blatant disobedience will always put His favor at risk. Until genuine repentance takes place, expect nothing different.

Please know, however, that I am not talking about your salvation being at risk. That is a completed deal. Your eternity is settled. It's one and done. But what is at risk is the extent of His favor on your life now.

* **How have you experienced blessings for obedience or hardships for disobedience?**

* **Read Hebrews 12:6. What is the basis for God's discipline? How does this connect with the consequences of our disobedience?**

Day Three

When I finished my time at college, I was planning to go right into youth ministry. My major had been Christian Thought/Christian Ministry. I had taken every Bible, ministry, and Christian education course offered. My heart was for working with youth and young adults, and I really thought that would be my career.

While I was in college, I accumulated $21,000 of student loan debt. My prayer all along, however, was that God would help me pay it off in three years. My goal following graduation was to be debt-free in three short years. So needless to say, it was necessary to find a job.

One day, I had an interview with Youth for Christ for a local opening. But because I didn't know if I'd get the job, I also applied for a position at a nearby, private golf club. An older friend had told me about an opening there for the summer months and encouraged me to apply.

On the very same day as my interview with Youth for Christ, I ran over to the golf club to drop off my application. But instead of simply taking my paperwork, the owner decided to interview me on the spot. What was supposed to be a two-minute detour in my day turned out to be an hour-long interview. And with just enough time, I then drove another hour away for the other appointment.

The YFC interview went really well. But even as I drove home, I began to feel the Lord directing me away from that job. So as much as I would have liked to say I was working in youth ministry, I couldn't take the YFC job. As it turned out though, the golf club offered me the position, and feeling peaceful about it, I accepted the job and began working there.

It was not the job I wanted. It wasn't the job for which I had prepared and planned. It wasn't a church position or ministry job next to those who loved Jesus and wanted to reach youth for Him. It was a golf club with people who loved golfing. I didn't know *what* God was doing! But I knew enough to be obedient and patient. And I remember my pastor at the time told me to bloom where I was planted.

So that is what I did. God had put me in that place. It was quite humbling not pursuing the field I had studied and for which I had obtained a degree. But He wanted me there, and I needed to find purpose and value while I was there. So I worked hard and made the best of things. Beyond that, I volunteered and got involved in unpaid youth ministry opportunities in my free time. I joined a ladies' Bible study group. And though I may not have understood the timing or the "why," I had to wait, and trust, and surrender because I knew God doesn't do anything without purpose, and I just had to be obedient.

At the end of the summer, the golf club asked me if I would stay on and work year-round even after they closed for the season. The most amazing thing was that they offered to pay off my student loans if I signed a contract and stayed for three years. And so I did. God was obviously using that job to answer my prayer and bring about blessings I couldn't have even imagined. And I believe His favor was present because I obeyed. Had I gone off on my own, I do not think those loans would have been paid off in three years. Was I glad I yielded? Absolutely!

His favor follows our obedience. What blessings might He bring into your life, what prayers might He answer as you walk in the way of His laws and follow *His* direction in your life? Obedience is the avenue of God's continued favor on our lives. It was true back in the days of the Israelites, and it is true still today.

Read 1 Samuel 4:3. What did the elders ask of each other?

> Obedience is the avenue of God's continued favor on our lives.

Why did the Lord bring defeat? Hmmm, let's think. Notice that the Israelites did ask the right question, "Why did the <u>Lord</u> bring defeat . . . ?" (emphasis added). It seems that they recognized God's control and power in the situation. But they asked the wrong person. They asked each other when they should have asked God.

Have you been in a situation where something happened, and you ran to this friend or that friend to talk, but you prolonged going to God over the problem? Something was pricking at your heart, but you just pushed it away because you didn't want to face having to submit to Him and His ways? Whew! Yeah, anyone else?

When something bad happens, do you find yourself running to friends first or to God? Why?

Read Psalm 81:8-16. What did God desire of His people?

But what did the people do instead?

Had they listened, what did God say would have happened (verses 14 -16)? List every result.

When we face any
defeat, our first
stop should be the
throne room.

I think somewhere, deep down, the elders of 1 Samuel 4 knew something was wrong. They must have known they were not right with the Lord otherwise they would have gone to Him immediately.

When we face any defeat, our first stop should be the throne room. I find it incredibly sad that the Israelites' defeat did not provoke them to seek the Lord. They didn't fast. They didn't pray or examine their hearts. They didn't offer a sacrifice.

Turn to Deuteronomy 28:15 and 25. Why were the Israelites being defeated by "their idol-worshipping neighbors?"[18] What had the elders forgotten about in regard to the terms of the covenant?

Israel had disobeyed God's law and was facing the consequences. But despite losing 4,000 men and instead of seeking the Lord for answers, what did they decide to do? They said, "Let's go to Shiloh and bring the ark here." They had won battles before with the ark, so why not now? But this was the difference: they were ignoring the context of those other battles and the most important things that Moses and Joshua did before battle. In Numbers 10:33-36 and Joshua 3-4 and 6, Moses and Joshua took the ark of the covenant into battle with them, but they had prepared hearts. They had prayed and were obeying precisely what God was telling them.

Why do you think the Israelites took the ark from Shiloh?

The people in 1 Samuel 4 were not seeking to obey nor glorify God, rather they were trying to provoke a victory. They were looking for something external to be done because they didn't want to look at the heart of the matter, which was their disobedience. They went with the thought that the ark would be the key to their deliverance.

Have you tried to provoke a particular outcome in a situation? Share an example.

The Israelites were tying God's favor to an object and not to obedience. Remember in the covenant, God presented blessings for obedience and curses for disobedience.

What do you think God's goal was with Israel when He explicitly laid out the curses for disobedience?

How do you handle God's discipline in your own life?

We cannot turn to the external in hopes of avoiding the internal when it comes to the things of God. Obedience starts in the heart. And that provokes this question, "What is in our hearts?" This is ritual vs. spirituality. Do we just go through the motion of obedience, or do we lay our hearts bare? Can we say, "Here I am. Teach me, mold me, whatever it takes to bring me closer to You"?

2 Timothy 3:5 speaks of having a form of godliness, but denying the power of it. There is power in a godly life. But let me ask you, does godliness just happen? No, it does not. I remember Beth Moore once making the point that if you can look at someone and say, "That is a godly woman," it most definitely did not happen by accident. If we want to live godly lives, it takes intention. There is work to be done if you and I want to address the heart and live a godly life that isn't just an appearance, but one that influences the world around us with power.

> We cannot turn to the external in hopes of avoiding the internal when it comes to the things of God. Obedience starts in the heart.

✣ **Do you make a deliberate attempt to live a godly life? What makes this ambition challenging? What are or can you be doing to be more successful?**

Read what Charles Spurgeon wrote about this:

> *We will attend to any outward duty, or to any external rite: but to bring our hearts into subjection to the divine will, to bow our minds to the Most High, and to serve the Lord our God with all our heart, and all our soul, the natural man abhors.*[19]

It can be so much easier to do something superficial, something external, to look the part of holy than it is to bring our hearts before God and obey.

Think about the Pharisees. They went over the top in trying not to break a commandment. They added hundreds of "elaborate but petty rules."[20] To observing the Sabbath alone, they added thirty-nine categories of forbidden activity in order to keep the Sabbath holy, even down to how far one could carry or move an object outside of one's house (which is 6 feet incidentally).[21]

The Pharisees made themselves appear all holy, but what did Jesus call them in Matthew 23:27-28? White-washed tombs. Pretty and clean on the outside, yet on the inside, they were like rotting flesh. But it was easier to follow a bunch of external rules than to do the hard work—to do the heart work. What do we do? Are we more inclined to do something external rather than making ourselves vulnerable before a holy God?

Just like the Pharisees, the Israelites in 1 Samuel 4 weren't interested in looking inward. Instead, they made an idol of the ark and thought that would be their ticket to victory. We'll see what happens next tomorrow.

✤ **Why is it easier to perform external acts than deal with the heart?**

Curious about this week's title?
We'll discover who Ichabod is
during our video at the end of the week.

Day Four

My daughter and I have a fun, little vegetable garden. It is a fenced-in garden that sits on the highest part of our property. And over the last four days, I have seen a snake in the garden three different times, along with his shed skin. Yes friends, the snake has made a home.

Now I know the snake could be helpful when it comes to hungry critters. But if the snake is allowed to continue in our garden, I can pretty much guarantee that my daughter's nightly watering of the garden is over. Her fear of snakes will win, and all the work will fall to me.

So when my husband comes home, he will have our blessing to find and dispose of said snake. Are my priorities misaligned here? Hmmm. I'll leave that for you to decide. But as we'll see today, our priorities are revealed in what we do and how we handle situations that arise. For the Israelites specifically, we will observe how their priorities affected whether or not they would choose to walk in the way of His laws.

Read 1 Samuel 4:4. To which city did they go?

_____

Who do we see there with the ark? _____ and

_____

Turn back to read about Eli's two sons in 1 Samuel 2:12-17, 22-25.

What were their offenses?

We can see from Scripture that Hophni and Phineas were two awful guys. They held no regard for the Lord whatsoever, but they continued to operate as priests. Why? Their father, the high priest Eli, did not remove them from the office. Eli made choices to preserve his family's occupation rather than be concerned for God's glory.

The high priest struggled with what to prioritize. He knew his sons were horrible, and he knew God was eventually going to deal with them because the Lord had told a prophet and Samuel about the downfall of Eli and his sons. But still, Eli did nothing about them. He went about in sin, carrying on as if all was well instead of confessing, repenting, and changing. When God convicts us of sin, we must prioritize humility, confession, and repentance, and not procrastinate on issues of obedience.

I was talking with a friend the other day, and I said something I shouldn't have. And later when I was thinking about it, God started moving on my heart that I shouldn't have said that particular thing. Now it would have been very easy to brush over. There was no harm done in it and I would have liked to just let the issue fade away without addressing it. But God wasn't about to let me. So the first chance I had, I told this friend that I shouldn't have spoken and I was wrong.

Whether it is our tongue, our thoughts, or our actions: we would be wise to move quickly and settle any issue of disobedience. Will we decide to push aside procrastination and instead, prioritize obedience?

What is God placing on your heart that you need to once and for all lay down and say, "Okay, this is it, Lord. You've been telling me this thing for a while now, and I am finally willing to come under your authority—to repent, to submit to Your will for my life, and stop this thing." Or maybe it is to start doing something that He put on your heart a long time ago, but you have been resistant. I hesitate at giving examples because I don't want you to simply think about a set group of illustrations. I want you to broaden the scope on "What, Lord, do you want me to deal with?" Whatever it might be, address it. Stop pushing it out of your mind.

> When God convicts us of sin, we must prioritize humility, confession, and repentance, and not procrastinate on issues of obedience.

Why is it easy to procrastinate on issues of obedience?

Is the Lord laying something on your heart and you need to prioritize your obedience to Him?

As we saw yesterday, the Israelites took the ark out of Shiloh and into danger without God's direction. And we will see that one act of disobedience leads to another.

Read 1 Samuel 4:5-9. What was going on in the Israelite camp?

The Israelites were whooping and hollering because the ark had arrived. But they confused a symbol of faith with the real presence of God. Which would you rather have—a symbol or the real presence? The Israelites may have had the ark, but the Lord had removed the glory from it; He was not present there.

And it makes me want to ask: Are there times when *we* carry Him around, acting like there is nothing wrong, like we are all good? Do we proudly carry our Bibles having the appearance of holiness, and yet inward, we're not yielding to and obeying the framework of His law? Have we forgotten who He is? Try as we might, we cannot make Him fit in a box. There is no success in going ahead without Him. It's easy for us to try, just as the Israelites did. But no amount of yelling and excitement will make up for the lack of His presence in our lives.

God was not there with them in camp, yet they felt confident because they had the ark. Feelings can be deceptive. The rowdy Israelites needed a little truth to come walking into camp.

It is easy for me to compare this to our professional football team, who doesn't have the greatest record. You can have the best fans, all the yelling, and all the excitement in the world, but if this year's team isn't any good, there won't be any victory. If your team isn't doing the right thing, no super bowl is coming your way. In the same manner, if your army isn't following God's ways and all you've got are over-excited troops, no amount of whooping and hollering is going to make a difference.

We need to know that our feelings may deceive us, but truth will not. The Israelites tried to manipulate God, but we cannot do that and walk in obedience. We can't "use" God for our own purposes. We can't say "God wants me to be happy so I can leave my family." "God wants me to be successful so if I cheat on this or that financially, it is ok." "God doesn't care if I tell little lies."

* **"I feel like this is the right thing to do." Why is this a dangerous statement?**

> Our feelings may deceive us, but truth will not.

Read Jeremiah 17:9. What does it reveal about our hearts?

Instead of looking to what we feel, we need to say to ourselves, "This is what God has to say on the matter, and that is the end of it." A good practice is to compare how we feel about a particular issue and see if it matches up with the Word of God.

* **Have you ever experienced your feelings being deceptive? Write down an example.**

47

How do you know what to trust?

So the Israelites are all pumped and excited, but what do we see happening a couple of miles away[22] with the Philistines?

Glance back to 1 Samuel 4:7-9. What change took place in the Philistine camp?

The Philistines became all nervous when they first heard the uproar in the Israelite camp. Had the Israelite God come into their camp? But all the Israelite hoopla ends up working against them because the Philistines just rile each other up and become more determined to fight. You see, the enemy is bolstered when we are walking in disobedience. Do you think Satan likes it when God's children are being disobedient? Absolutely. We just made his job so much easier. And we shouldn't want any part of that.

Close by writing a prayer asking God to help you recognize truth and prioritize obedience.

Day Five

Let's jump right in! Please read 1 Samuel 4:10-11. Record what happened in these verses.

Once again, the Israelites are defeated. But this time, the slaughter was even greater. In fulfillment of prophesy, Phineas and Hophni died. And worst of all, the ark was captured and taken into enemy hands.

This reminds me of James 1:14-15. Let's turn there now. Fill in the missing words.

". . . but each person is tempted when they are dragged away by their own evil _____ and enticed. Then, after _____ has conceived, it gives birth to _____; and _____, when it is full-grown, gives birth to _____."

There are two different Greek words translated here as "give birth" in the NIV. They are tiktó (tik'-to) and apokueó (ap-ok-oo-eh'-o). Tiktó means to beget, bring forth,[23] bear, be born.[24] And apokueó means to give birth to.[25] Both words provide us with this image of birthing something. After desire has conceived, sin is birthed. Likewise, sin then gives birth to something else. What does Scripture tell us it births? Death. Something is going to die.

When we walk in continued disobedience, be fully aware that something is going to die. What happens when you ignore your garden and when you don't take care of the weeds? The garden becomes taken over, right? And what hap-

> When we walk in continued disobedience, be fully aware that something is going to die.

pens to the plants? They get choked. They don't have room to grow and become healthy plants. And in some cases, they outright die.

Maybe there is a fruit in our life that God wants to develop, and we are letting the weeds take over completely. Maybe there is a blessing the Lord was going to give us, but when we walk in disobedience, that blessing just dies. Or maybe it is simply that the closeness, that intimacy that we have enjoyed with the Lord, is going to die for a while until we repent and get our act together.

In this case, 30,000 men died, and the ark was taken. "Never in the history of Israel had the ark of God ever fallen into enemy hands."[26] Remember this was where the glory, the presence of God, dwelled when it was in the tabernacle.

Read I Samuel 4:12-18. That same day, where did the Benjamite run?

Oh boy. Here we go. From Ebenezer, where the battle took place, to Shiloh was about 20 miles away and mostly uphill.[27] This Benjamite made the trip in one day. And notice that the Scriptures tell us that his clothes were torn, and he had dust on his head. These were "common signs of grief and despair."[28] The Jews would tear their clothes and throw dust on their heads as visible signs of anguish.

The Benjamite delivers the news to Shiloh, and we see that the whole town sent up a cry. Remember, this was Israel's center for worship. The absence of the ark was a great loss for Shiloh.

I find it especially interesting that in verse 13, we see Eli sitting on a chair by the side of the road watching. What did we learn about him in verse 15?

Yes, he was blind! Eli was blind both physically and we could say spiritually as well. Yet, he is *watching* for news. We can see that he feared for the ark of God. It's just too bad that he didn't fear the God of the ark as well.

A lack of fear for God is a dangerous place to be. Had Eli feared God, he would have dismissed his sons as priests, but he did not. Had he feared God, he might have directed the people to submit to the Lord. Had he feared God, Eli might have stopped the ark from going into battle.

Look up Psalm 85:9. Write it below.

Please know that I am not talking about an unhealthy fear of God, like a child toward an abusive type of parent. The Bible speaks of the fear of the Lord as the beginning of knowledge (Proverbs 1:7). This fear is a reverence, a proper position of humility before a holy God. It is seeing God for who He is and recognizing His supreme authority, His vast power, His perfect judgment, His masterful wisdom, and it offers a respect that influences our actions. If we want His glory to dwell in our land, we need to have a healthy fear of Him, of who He is, and of that for which He is capable.

> A lack of fear for God is a dangerous place to be.

Read Revelation 15:4. What question is being asked?

✦**What difference does having a fear of God make in our lives?**

What exactly should we fear?

✣ **How can our view of God relate to our obedience?**

The Benjamite told the town first, and then, he told Eli. Notice the order in which the Benjamite shared the news with Eli. He told him that Israel fled from the Philistines, that the army suffered great loss, that Eli's sons (Hophni and Phineas) had died, and then as if to save the most damaging for last, he reported that the ark of God had been captured.

And that is where we will pick up in the video lesson. You won't want to miss what happens next. I can't wait to meet with you!

Birthing an Ichabod

The wife of Phineas names her son Ichabod, meaning the _____ has departed from Israel.

No area of disobedience is worth _____ the divine presence of God in our lives.

A _____ obedient life brings great glory to God.

"Live such good lives among the pagans that, though they may accuse you of doing wrong, they may see your good deeds and _____ God on the day he visits us."—1 Peter 2:12

Video lessons are available at KristenTiber.com/GreaterGloryVideos.

Week Three
Scattered Seed

" . . . bearing fruit in every good work,
growing in the knowledge of God,
being strengthened with all power
according to his glorious might
so that you may have great endurance and patience, and giving joyful
thanks to the Father . . ."

COLOSSIANS 1:10B-12A

Day One

Have you ever thought that our culture does not know how to wait? Take a moment to consider this.

> ✧ **Imagine you met a stranger who asked about our culture's ability to be patient. If you had to prove to a stranger that our culture does not know how to wait, what evidence might you give?**

We live in a fast-paced, tech-saturated world with everything at our fingertips. We have grown accustomed to instant updates, immediate notifications, and every answer only seconds away from a voice-commanded search. We have Instant Pots to make our food cook faster. We have Amazon Prime to deliver in two days. Although, sometimes you can get same-day delivery, which seriously blows this country girl's mind. Even when we are sitting and waiting, we can whip out our phones to fill the void in our down time. No longer do we have to simply wait.

But with all this instant gratification, I often wonder if our hearts have followed our culture's pattern when it comes to the things of God? As Christians, there are times when we must wait, and that waiting isn't always easy. Whether it's waiting for a situation to be resolved, a restored relationship, the right job, the right person to marry, a diagnosis, or navigating physical and emotional pain—waiting without a healthy, biblical perspective can be disappointing, sad, and exhausting to say the very least.

Have our hearts followed our culture's pattern when it comes to the things of God?

What happens when things don't move as fast as we would like; when God doesn't move on our timeline?

How do you feel about waiting?

Let's look back to Isaiah 26:8. "Yes, LORD, walking in the way of your laws, <u>we wait for you</u>; your name and renown are the desire of our hearts" (emphasis added). This week, we are looking at the snapshot of patience—those times and seasons in our lives when we need to wait for God. And we'll see how our patience can bring God glory.

For the last 15 years now, I have had back issues. It's a situation I have grown accustomed to, and it doesn't usually phase me. I know what I can and cannot do—and as much as possible, I just try to operate along those lines.

The year that Dan herniated two of his discs, however, was a bad year. Because Dan was being so careful with his back, I started doing things I probably shouldn't have been doing—lifting heavy items, moving big things. Tasks I would have normally asked him to do. But I didn't want to ask. I really wanted his back to have the chance to heal. So as that particular summer went on, my pain level just grew and grew. And I remember for the first time since the very beginning of my back issues, simply wanting to have surgery. I had always hesitated, not wishing to go through such a big and risky surgery. But now, I was finally ready to face it. Bring it on because the pain was constant, and it was great.

We started looking around to determine the doctor I should see. A coworker of Dan's gave him a name. It was the name of his surgeon, a man of whom he couldn't speak more highly. I asked the Lord for confirmation that this was the man I should see, and within 24 hours, we received the same name from a close friend. I felt great comfort about going to see him so I made the appointment. It turned out that he was the head of orthopedics for one of the two major hospital systems in the area. I like going right to the top so I felt very good about this appointment and was confident of God's leading.

I had a new MRI taken, gathered all of my documents, and headed to his office mid-morning on the day of the appointment. Dan came from work and met me there. We waited together in the exam room. I had such a nervous, anxious feeling. The doctor walked in with his entourage, and he put my MRI up on the board.

And in the next few minutes, he explained to me that I was not a candidate for surgery. He couldn't guarantee that my pain was just from the herniated disc. He couldn't guarantee that snipping the disc would fix me. And given the risk therefore, he believed surgery was not the best option for me.

I started to phase out for a moment because Dan started asking about his own back. We laugh now about how from that point on, he just took over the appointment. As they talked, I sat there on that exam table, on top of the crinkly paper, feet hanging down, fighting back tears . . . because this was supposed to be my ticket out. This was going to be the answer to all the pain I was experiencing.

We thanked the doctor and left. Dan hopped in his car to head back to work, and when I got to my minivan and sat down, I just cried. Really cried. All my hope for relief had been tied up in that surgery. And now I was faced with the reality that it wasn't even a consideration.

What do you do in those moments when hopes are crushed? When you're living and waiting through a tough season? What do you do when you feel like you can no longer stand? When you just need some peace or a sense of normalcy and there is no end in sight?

Well this week, we're going to do the first thing that we can always do—go right to the Word of God. We're going to plant ourselves in a passage that will help teach us what God wants us to know about patience.

Before we start reading though, I would like you to take a moment and jot down what it is you are waiting for right now. Maybe you are needing to be patient through a situation, maybe you're waiting for direction, or there is something in particular for which you find yourself in the position of biding time. Take a moment and write it down. And if you don't have anything right now, that is okay. You can work on what we're learning for a future season in which you do have to wait.

✦ **What is it you are waiting for?**

We are going to turn now to James 5. Right here, packed into five little verses, James shares with us three examples of patience. And each of these three examples teach us different things.

You should know that James is talking about being patient for the Lord's coming; and well, isn't that the ultimate for which we wait? One commentator said that we "patiently endure the sufferings of the present life in view of the future prospect of the coming of the Lord."[29] These lessons on patience can be applied to whatever we are facing in this present life as we wait for the Lord's return.

Read James 5:7-11. James gives three examples of those being patient. List them below.

1.

2.

3.

Read these verses again and then take a few moments to outline this passage. The practice of outlining a passage can be very helpful in finding hidden information and discovering the gems of a text. You may choose to create your own outline or use the format below.

James' Initial Instruction (v7):

First Example (v7):

Waits for (v7):

Secondary Instruction (v8):

Warning (v9):

Second Example (v10):

Patient through (v10):

Third Example (v11):

Commended for (v11):

Attributes of the Lord Shared (v11):

What stands out to you after outlining the passage?

This week, we will look more in depth at each example James provides and see what we can learn about being patient in our own lives for the ultimate purpose of bringing glory to God. I wonder which will be your favorite? I'll tell you mine at the end of the week.

Day Two

My daughter, Anna, is at camp this week so in the evening, I have fully taken over the responsibility of watering the garden. Each time I am up on that hill, I am surprised at how absolutely delighted I feel to see everything growing. We have yet to pluck a ripe tomato, but the fruit is there, nearly ready. And to date, we have gathered a couple of strawberries, a few zucchini, one cucumber, and a number of jalapeno peppers, which my husband enjoys on his burgers, in his eggs or in any type of random concoction. Just don't use the same knife on your beans after he cuts the jalapeno. Green beans with a kick, anyone?

My daughter's passion for her garden has increased as the fruit has become visible, and the harvest has begun. But as the case would be with most ten-year olds, the first part of the season did not do much to keep her interest. Can you relate?

Today, let's take a look at James' example of patience in the farmer. Reread James 5:7. For what does Scripture tell us the farmer waits?

The *Bible Exposition Commentary* shares, "Jewish farmers would plow and sow in what to us are the autumn months. The 'early rain' would soften the soil. The 'latter rain' would come in the early spring (our February/March) and help to mature the harvest."[30]

Think about the patience that a farmer must have. He plants the seed and then has to wait to see anything happen. He has to wait while the seed opens and sends down roots, while it sprouts a stem, while it forms its leaves and its flowers, and then grows and grows and matures until finally the crop, the fruit, is produced.

In our homeschool this year, we did a side study on botany. It really was fascinating to see how plants grow. I had no idea what God packs in a seed that serves a purpose to grow and produce fruit. He is so wise!

Have you ever planted seeds? Does the flower or the fruit happen immediately? In the first year of Anna's garden, we bought all of our plants. We didn't start anything from seed. We started with cute, little plants, and even with that advantage, the first fruits seemed to take forever to make their appearance.

A farmer waits a long time for his seed to produce fruit, and he is patient about it. How can he do this? Why can he wait so patiently? Because the farmer knows that the waiting is not in vain. He knows that radical transformation is taking place below the surface of the soil. From the farmer, we learn that incredible change is taking place even though we cannot see it.[31]

When we are in a season of waiting, God is still moving. Don't ever doubt it. There is change going on that is unseen. This reminds me of a verse in 2 Corinthians.

> The farmer knows that waiting is not in vain. Incredible change is happening even though he cannot see it.

Read 2 Corinthians 5:7. What do we learn from this verse?

The truth from this verse is that we cannot simply live, walk, or trust God by only looking at what is visible to our eyes. What would happen if the farmer did that? He would quickly be discouraged, plow over the field and start over. No, the farmer knows that change is happening even when he cannot see it.

✣ **Why do you think it can be hard to be patient when change is not visible?**

Can you look at your situation—whatever it was that you wrote down on Day One—and say, "Hey, something is happening right now even though I can't see it?" Would you tell and encourage yourself that God is moving even if you can't see how at this very moment? Your situation might be sitting in the dirt right now, but God is at work even so.

✣ **How might the Lord be moving at this very moment in your situation?**

Allow me to suggest to you that it is very possible the biggest work going on when we cannot see anything is right inside our very own hearts. The Lord is using our situation to teach us, to mold us, and to refine us. There is transformation going on, and He is using this time of waiting to transform you and me for His glory.[32]

> **Read 2 Corinthians 3:18 and fill in the blank. "And we all, who with unveiled faces contemplate the Lord's glory, are being transformed into _____ with ever-increasing glory, which comes from the Lord, who is the Spirit."**

The Greek word used in the beginning of our passage by James when he says "Be patient" is makrothumeo (mak-roth-oo-meh'-o), and it means to be longsuffering, to have patience, and to patiently endure.[33] *Thayer's Greek Lexicon* puts the definition this way, "to persevere patiently and bravely in enduring misfortunes and troubles."[34]

How are you doing on that? Are you enduring patiently and bravely?

This is the same word used in Hebrews 6:15 that says after Abraham waited patiently, he received what was promised. I like the KJV on this when it says, "After he had <u>patiently endured</u>, he obtained the promise" (emphasis added).[35] Patience is about endurance. We're in it for the long haul. This isn't just the 100 meter dash, this is the 26 mile marathon.

How can you better endure with patience?

Now, what else does the farmer know? The farmer knows the result is worth the wait. Last year, when Anna cut her very first cucumber and plucked her first tomato, you can imagine how utterly excited she was. Her smile was ear to ear, and what fun and joy we had each time we picked something from that little garden. It was rough taking care of it and waiting, but it was worth the wait. And so it will be as you wait on God.

Write a prayer asking God to help you wait as the farmer does.

The farmer
knows the result
is worth the wait.

Day Three

Now that we can recognize that the wait is worth it, what do we do as we wait? Are we to do nothing as we wait to see what God is doing? With Anna's garden, we had to fertilize it frequently and water it every night. Last year, we had to deal with the grossest tomato worms that looked like freak show caterpillars with this pointy red horn and oozed green slime when squashed (as my son found out). We had to spray neem oil to deal with mold that was growing on many of the leaves of the plants on the ground. This year, we discovered something called a tortoise beetle enjoying the leaves of our tomato plants. There is no doubt about it. Having a garden is so much work!

Do you think the farmer just kicked up his feet and waited for the field to produce its fruit? No. He stayed busy. He worked the farm. He took care of the fields. He did the hard work!

Being patient doesn't mean we can kick back and stop living the Christian life.

What should we be doing while we wait?

Send your roots down deep in the things of God. Stay faithful. Dig into the Word. Stay busy serving in the Kingdom. I think one of the worst things we can do when we are in this position of waiting is to isolate ourselves—and allow our world to become so small that all our problems end up looking bigger. No, we need to get out and stay active, building our faith and serving others in the body of Christ.

Look at James 5:8 in the *Amplified Bible*: "You too, be patient; strengthen your hearts [keep them energized and firmly committed to God], because the coming of the Lord is near."[36]

It takes work to keep your heart energized and firmly committed to God. But do the work. It is so worth it! And really, we know what we need to do to keep our hearts committed to God, right? We need to be getting in the Word, surrounding ourselves with other believers, and developing a rich prayer life. What I hope is that the things I do when seasons are easy become habitual. Then when I'm in the season of waiting and having to endure, those practices are second nature, and I'm just doing what I know to do.

Many years ago, my cousin Cherise told me a story of when she was at JOANN's buying fabric. This was back when she had just had her first or second child. For her, that was the season of rocking babies. (Although, I suppose she is still in that phase today with her fifth child just having turned one.)

Cherise was in the fabric line, waiting to have her material cut. And while she was waiting for her turn, she was rocking. Well at some point, she looked down and realized it wasn't a baby she was holding. She was rocking the bolt of fabric . . . back and forth. She was just doing what she was accustomed to doing. Rocking her babies was so habitual for her that even when she was out and about standing and waiting, she just kept rocking.

"Be joyful in hope, patient in affliction, faithful in prayer."

—ROMANS 12:12

When you are waiting, keep rocking—whether it is a baby, a bolt of fabric or your prayer life. Keep moving. Keep standing. Keep fighting. Keep living the faithful life.

Now, before we see what James shares next, let's recap what we learned about the farmer. The farmer recognizes that change is taking place even when it cannot be seen. He knows the wait is worth it, and he knows to keep moving while he is waiting.

Read James 5:9. What does James warn against?

_____

James says not to grumble against one another because the Judge is at the door. Do you ever feel frustrated about being patient and find it just opens you up to a bad attitude, and you are quick to complain? No? Me neither. Ever.

Look at the following verses and note what they say or how they relate to complaining:

Ephesians 4:29

Philippians 2:12-18

1 Thessalonians 5:16-18

When we need to exercise patience, we would be wise to see that the time of waiting doesn't become a gripe session. James puts us on notice that our grumbling will bring judgement from God. After all, the Judge is at the door. Any complaint is ultimately against Him.

Instead of complaints flying out of our mouths, let's consider Psalm 40:1-5. What does David say he did in verse 1?

List all the ways the Lord responded in verses 1-2.

In verse 3, what do we learn that God put in David's mouth?

And what was the result?

�֍ **Why is it important that we don't allow complaining and grumbling to creep into our times of waiting?**

At the college I attended, my three friends and I have a brick etched with our first names in the courtyard behind the student union. Each time we visit, we find that brick among all of the others. You'd think after so many years, we would know exactly where to look but it always seems to take a little longer than it should. Also in my small town, my family has a brick with our first names found on the historic town square. Listed on both bricks along with our names is the reference "Psalm 40:5." This has always been one of my favorite verses.

> *"Many, Lord my God, are the wonders you have done,*
> *the things you planned for us.*
> *None can compare with you;*
> *were I to speak and tell of your deeds,*
> *they would be too many to declare."*
>
> —PSALM 40:5

Even when we are waiting, our hearts can overflow with thanks and gratitude, with awe and songs of praise for the God we serve. We are less likely to give in to a grumbling spirit when wonder fills our heart for who God is. Keep your focus on Jesus.

✢ **How can having an awe for God help keep you from grumbling?**

Day Four

Please start today by rereading James 5:10 and making note of what James said.

As we continue to focus this week on our passage in James 5, I want to share with you a little bit of background on this five-chapter book. The author, James, was a leader in the Jerusalem church, and this letter was written to Jewish believers. One thing I find incredibly cool is that this letter from James may have been the earliest of the New Testament writings.[37] I believe that this James was the half-brother of Jesus. Being Jewish himself and knowing his Jewish audience so well, James was able to make a quick reference to the prophets in verse 10, and his readers would have been fully able to make the connection because they knew their history. For us however, we may need to dive in just a bit more to discover what was so special about the patience of the prophets.

The prophets were God's mouthpieces. If the priests represented the people to God, then the prophets represented God to the people. They gave the Word of the Lord to kings, to nations, to pagan people, and to God's very own people. And whether it was a call for repentance, reform, and a return to God, or they were prophesying about coming blessings or curses, the prophets were doing the work to which God called them. But, they still suffered. (By the way, this squelches the extreme view of that time that all suffering was a result of sin.)

✢ Let's look up the following verses and find out what some of the
prophets were going through. Fill in the blanks with what you learn.

The prophets were _____ (Acts 7:52).

Jezebel threatened Elijah's _____ which put him on
the run (1 Kings 19:1-3).

Micaiah was imprisoned and given only _____ and
_____ (1 Kings 22:27).

Elisha was _____ (2 Kings 2:23).

Zechariah was _____ to _____
(2 Chronicles 24:20-21).

The prophets were told to stop _____ and only to
share "pleasant things" (Isaiah 30:10). Yet, they did not stop.

Jeremiah was a prophet for more than 40 years during what
was likely the darkest period of Judah's history. He proclaimed
"messages of doom,"[38] called for Judah's reform, and pronounced
judgement to other nations.

During that time, he was threatened with _____
(Jeremiah 26:7-8).

He was _____ and _____
(Jeremiah 37:15-16).

He was thrown into a _____ (Jeremiah 38:6).

Jeremiah was bound with _____ (Jeremiah 40:1).

Jeremiah knew his words from the Lord brought insult, reproach, and suffering, but to what do we see him compare his need to speak forth? Jeremiah said that His word was like a _____ shut up in his bones (Jeremiah 20:9). He could not hold in the message of the Lord. And so, he endured.

The prophets had to patiently endure persecution and wait for victory. They had to wait for God to move and fulfill what He had spoken. They were mistreated, rejected, and forsaken by the people, but even though they suffered, God still showed great care for them. From elsewhere in Scripture, we know that He took care of Elijah, he fed Jeremiah, he delivered Ezekiel and Daniel. But why did the prophets have to endure such hardship?

Here is what one Bible commentator said, "It is so that their lives might back up their messages. The impact of a faithful, godly life carries much power. We need to remind ourselves that our patience in times of suffering is a testimony to others around us."[39] The prophets, despite the suffering, kept witnessing![40] From the prophets, we learn that our patience will be a witness to a watching world trained in instant gratification and reared to run from adversity.

Our patience will be a witness to a watching world trained in instant gratification and reared to run from adversity.

Does your life back up your message?

I like this definition of patience: "the capacity to accept or tolerate delay, trouble, or suffering without getting upset or angry."[41] Do you think this will stand out in our culture? Absolutely! Will it then bring glory to God as we exercise patience in our lives? You bet!

Let's wrap up today by reading the following passage from Paul's letter to the Colossians. Please underline any key words or phrases you find.

For this reason, since the day we heard about you, we have not stopped praying for you. We continually ask God to fill you with the knowledge of his will through all the wisdom and understanding that the Spirit gives, so that you may live a life worthy of the Lord and please him in every way: bearing fruit in every good work, growing in the knowledge of God, being strengthened with all power according to his glorious might so that you may have great endurance and patience, and giving joyful thanks to the Father, who has qualified you to share in the inheritance of his holy people in the kingdom of light. For he has rescued us from the dominion of darkness and brought us into the kingdom of the Son he loves, in whom we have redemption, the forgiveness of sins. (Colossians 1:9-14)

✤ **What is God laying on your heart as we remember the patience of the prophets?**

Day Five

The third and final example James brings to our attention is Job. Job was a godly man who had so many things going for him, including God's favor and His pleasure. But in the book of Job, we see that Satan came before God and accused Job of only being faithful because of God's blessing on his life.

Before we turn to Job, let's refresh our memory with what James said about Job in James 5:11. What did James praise about Job?

Now read Job 1:1-5. What do we learn about Job?

Read Job 1:6-12. What took place in these verses?

God allowed Satan to sift Job—taking away the blessings, even to the point of causing him great physical ailment (as allowed in Job 2:3-8). Job lost his animals and herds, his children, his wealth, most of his servants, his house and was even covered from the top of his head to the bottom of his feet with painful sores. Yet, he patiently endured and stood his ground in believing God.

And when we see James start verse 11 with how blessed are those who have persevered (or patiently endured)—this is the Greek verb humpomeno (hoop-om-en'-o), and it is very closely related to the noun James uses in his next breath to describe Job's perseverance, hupomoné (hoop-om-on-ay'). The word, humpomeno, means to stay behind, to await, endure. The usage according to *Strong's Concordance* is to remain behind, to stand your ground.[42] The reason I am sharing this is—when we are in the midst of waiting, when we are in a situation that is uncomfortable, when we want to run and our heart is questioning so many things—we need to stand our ground. We can't give in to defeat and despair.

From Job, we learn that patience involves standing your ground. And that is what we see Job doing.

What did Job say after experiencing such a great number of losses? Turn to Job 1:21-22. Record what you find.

Isn't that spectacular? He still praises God. He still blesses the Lord. He remains steadfast and shows great endurance. Even into what we see throughout the rest of the book of Job, he stood his ground.

Another thing we need to take note of is what triggered this particular time of testing for Job.

Patience involves standing your ground.

Was it his disobedience? _____

Was it waiting for the prophetic to be fulfilled? _____

This whole ordeal began because of Satan's attack on Job.

We have to realize that as followers of Christ, Satan is going to attack us as well. I'm pretty sure Satan likes this instant world we live in. When we are used to it, when we are accustomed to having everything without delay and then we face a trial or hardship and God takes longer than we'd like—we might start to question Him. "Is God really good? Is He real? Is what He says true? Did He really say . . . ?" And with that last question, we're right back to the garden. "Did God really say . . . ?" (Genesis 3:1). There will be times in our lives when our waiting is because we are facing spiritual attack, and we need to stand firm and persevere.

Can you think of a time when you were facing a spiritual attack?

Let's consider Daniel's situation in Daniel 10. At the beginning of this chapter, Daniel was given a vision of war, which he didn't understand. So he mourned, he ate no choice food, no meat, no wine, and he didn't use any lotions for a period of twenty-one days. And where we will start reading is after these twenty-one days, the angel arrived and spoke to Daniel.

Read Daniel 10:12-14. What was the reason the angel gave for his delay?

Why did Daniel have to wait for the answer? We see here that from the first day Daniel set his mind to gain understanding and to humble himself, his words were heard by God, and an angel was sent with an answer. But what stopped him? The prince of Persia, a fallen angel that had some kind of authority over the physical kingdom of Persia, got in the way. There was a spiritual battle in the heavenlies. Scripture tells us that Michael, who is Israel's archangel (a warrior-angel), had to come and help this messenger angel break through.

There will be instances in our lives when the delayed answer, or the resolution of an issue is because there is warring in the heavenlies. Daniel prayed and fasted for twenty-one days, and that was when the angel then arrived. We need to stand our ground patiently and bravely, and sometimes we need to pray and fast in order to see breakthrough.

When we look at the book of James as a whole, James has one central theme. The book is about Christian maturity.[43] James wanted to see the Jewish readers live their faith. Whether it was having patience in difficulties, controlling the tongue, or not being consumed with material goods, James wanted to see his readers grow up in their faith. And regarding patience, James not only concerned himself with it here in chapter 5, but also in chapter 1. He saw patience as an important part of Christian maturity.

You may already be familiar with the fruit of the Spirit. The commonly quoted list of Christian attributes is found in Galatians 5:22. They are love, joy, peace, patience, kindness, goodness, faithfulness, gentleness, and self-control. Did you catch the fruit of patience? Draw a circle around it. Patience is a fruit of the Spirit.

Let's look at John 15:5-8. How do we bear fruit according to verse 5?

To what end do we bear fruit and show ourselves to be His disciples (verse 8)?

Yes, my friends. We bring the Father glory by bearing fruit, by exhibiting patience in our lives. How are you doing today with the fruit of patience? Is it time to tend the garden?

Scattered Seed

God will always fill our seasons of waiting with greater _____.

Even when we face the unknown, we know the One on whom we wait, and we know He is _____ and _____ to the end.

"Diaspora" means a _____ .

"Waiting is not about what you get at the end of the wait; it's about what you _____ as you wait."—Paul David Tripp

Video lessons are available at KristenTiber.com/GreaterGloryVideos.

Week Four

Fuel for the Fire

"For where your treasure is,
there your heart be also."

MATTHEW 6:21

Day One

Wow, we are charging right though! Here we are with only two more weeks of study, and I am loving every minute with you. How I pray God would tune our ears to hear His voice, fix our eyes to see our everyday in light of eternity, and set our lips with a new hymn of praise.

As we start this fourth week, I would like to ask you to take a moment and think about the following:

Over the years, what have been the desires of your heart? What have been the things you wanted out of life?

All kinds of ideas flood my mind. Desires for marriage, kids, work, the salvation of friends and family, and if I'm going to be honest, visiting Disney World. Oh, how I love that place.

When we look at the desires of our heart, an important question to consider is: How do our desires line up with God's? Yes, I would like to go to Disney World every other month, but is that what God wants for me? No, I don't think so.

In a *Desiring God* article, Jon Bloom sorted personal dreams into three categories: things we desire to become, things we desire to achieve, and things we desire to possess. [44] Think of all the children who dream of what they will be when they grow up. Our desires may involve what we want to *become* such as a teacher, a nurse, a wife, a mother, a business leader, or an entrepreneur.

How do the desires of your heart line up with God's?

✢**What did you want to be when you grew up?**

Our dreams and desires can also involve things we want to *possess* like a house, a great piece of property, an exquisite library, a set amount of money in the bank, or an awesome car like a mini-van . . . okay, so not everyone dreams of a minivan, and that just baffles me. Hello, automatic doors!

Our desires may also be things we want to *accomplish*: a goal we set, a level of notoriety at work, a certain degree, or financial accomplishment like becoming debt-free or saving up for a purchase. Dreams and desires can be many things. Let's face it, we probably even have desires for our kids and grandkids—who they will become or what they may accomplish.

Many of these things can be great desires of our heart. In the *Desiring God* article though, the author astutely noted, "All of those dreams might be wonderful, or they might be wicked. The determining factor is what desires are fueling the dreams."[45]

As followers of Christ, we need to be looking at what is fueling our dreams and desires. So this week, we are going to put on our Kingdom glasses. As part of God's Kingdom, how do all these things we hope for, wish for, and desire play into Kingdom living? Are there some biblical principles we can use to bring balance to what our heart tells us it wants? And last, how does this connect to God's glory?

What is a current desire of your heart?

> As followers of Christ, we need to be looking at what is fueling our dreams and desires.

What do you think is fueling that dream?

This week, we are going to look at three people and ask two questions of each: What did the person desire? What fueled his desire? (You'll find a chart on page 100 to help track these answers throughout the week.) We will also consider what we can learn from each individual.

So, let's turn to Acts 8. Please read Acts 8:9-13.

The first individual we are going to look at is _____ the Sorcerer.

Record every detail Scripture provides about Simon:

When we think about what it is Simon desires, we can see right from the start of our passage in verse 9 that Simon is after self-promotion. Scripture tells us that he is boasting and telling the people that he was "someone great." Now I'm not sure, but the last time I checked, if you need to tell someone you are great, we already know something is amiss. In addition, the Samaritans thought that Simon possessed the power of God. Several commentaries note that this is a claim to deity.[46] And it seems that Simon ate this up.

What did Simon desire?

One trend I notice with young people and all their posting on social media is that many want to be someone great like Simon. They want large followings, massive likes, and scads of shares. They want attention and notoriety. They want to be noticed. Do you ever feel this way?

What fueled Simon's desire? (Don't forget to add your answers to the chart on page 100.)

Do you think Simon wanted fame and attention for the benefit of someone else? Was he doing all this for someone else's glory? No, he wanted it for his own glory. Living in the Kingdom, we need to be cautious that we don't fall into this trap. Scripture is clear about seeking our own glory.

Turn to Psalm 115:1. What is the psalmist's approach to seeking glory?

Read Isaiah 42:8. What do we learn from this verse?

If there is glory to be had, who should get it? God. God should receive all glory in anything we do. Boastful talk and self-promotion have no place in Kingdom living. Instead, we need to give all glory to our King. This is the first thing we can learn from Simon.

Everything we are and everything we have is because of what the Lord has given us. If we have a house to live in and a car to drive, it is ultimately because it has come from the hand of God. Everything we have is His and is from Him. Therefore, we shouldn't be boastful. If there is any crown in this life, we should be like the twenty-four elders in Revelation 4. What did they do with their crowns? They laid their crowns at the feet of Him who sat on the throne. And they said, in verse 11, "You are worthy, our Lord and God, to receive <u>glory</u> and honor and power, for you created all things, and by your will they were created and have their being" (emphasis added).

Now, does God plant dreams in our hearts that might lead to attention or success (whether in the workplace or elsewhere)? Absolutely! But our goal in pursuing our dreams should never be for our own self-promotion. Our goal should be to serve and be used by God. To His glory!

> Boastful talk and self-promotion have no place in Kingdom living. Instead, we need to give all glory to our King.

Thoughts to conclude today's study:

✣ **When you look at the world in which we live, what do you think fuels most dreams and desires?**

✣ **Do you think Christians can become wrapped up in worldly desires? How do we avoid the snare and keep our focus in the right place?**

Day Two

At the end of yesterday's passage, we saw that Philip came to Samaria and preached the good news of the Kingdom of God and of Jesus. As a result, people were converted and baptized. Simon also believed, was baptized and then followed Phillip as well.

Look back at Acts 8:13. To what does Scripture tell us Simon was attracted?

Can you picture the scene? Here is this magician looking for attention and admiration from the crowds. Then Philip comes along, preaching and performing miracles. His wonderous acts (done for the glory of God) were greater than what Simon could do. And this amazed him. So Simon began following Philip everywhere.

Read Acts 8:14-23. Who came from Jerusalem? What did they find?

The Jerusalem church had heard of the large number of conversions in Samaria, and they sent Peter and John. Given the tension between Samaritans and Jews, this shouldn't be a surprise. The Jerusalem church wanted to confirm that the conversions were genuine.

Now what is an unusual side note is that the people had not yet received the Holy Spirit. Usually in Scripture, we see the receiving of the Spirit to be immediate upon belief. But not here. Some speculate that "God delayed the giving of the Spirit [until Peter and John came] for the sake of Christian unity: (1) to confirm to the Samaritans that they were one with the Jerusalem church and (2) to confirm to the Jerusalem church that the Samaritans were indeed saved."[47]

Peter and John came and prayed for the people, laying their hands on them and Simon saw that the Holy Spirit was given in this case through the laying on of the apostles' hands. Thinking of how it could benefit him, Simon wanted to buy the ability. He wanted that same power. As one scholar put it, he "treats the gift of the Spirit as one more power to acquire and exploit for financial gain."[48]

But what happened? Peter rebuked him for thinking that the gift of God could be bought.

✢ **In verse 21, what did Peter tell Simon was not right?**

Does this imply that Peter meant Simon's faith was not authentic, that it was rather a self-serving faith because of the consuming interest in miracles? It sure seems that way, especially if this is the same man whom church history calls Simon Magnus, the magician, who went on to become a heretic and the founder of a Gnostic sect who opposed the church in Rome.[49]

But what can we learn by what Peter says to Simon? We can know that our personal desires are measured by what is in our heart. God sees inside. He sees the heart. All motives are laid bare before Him. We can ask ourselves if our motives are pure. Is our desire to be used by God? Is it to serve Him wherever He has us—whether at work, at church, or with our families, our husbands, or our children? What is in our heart, driving what we say and do? Are we conniving? Are we selfish? Do we go about getting what we want in a deceptive manner? What is in our heart?

When Anna was about four years old, she and Peter (two years older) were at my mom's house. The two of them were eating lunch on her front brick walk. My mom had carried out a sweet little kids' table and two chairs, so they could enjoy their food outside. As lunch progressed, my mom brought out a little plate with two brownies and set it down on the table. You should know that one of these brownies was clearly bigger than the other.

Anna saw the two brownies of differing size and said to Peter, "Peter, I know you like to finish your food first, so it is okay with me if you eat the smaller brownie." He didn't go for it.

> Our personal desires are measured by what is in our heart.

But that girl thought and rephrased, and on the third time, Peter picked up and ate the smaller brownie. And Anna feasted on the big one. Now, what was in her heart? She sounded like she was looking out for Peter. But really, she wanted the bigger brownie and she said what had to be said to motivate Peter to choose the small one.

Let's do a little heart check. When it comes to your dreams and desires, is your heart right before God? Are your motives pure? Do you have desires that need to be realigned?

There is something else in the passage I would like you to notice. Closer to the beginning of chapter eight, we saw that the people were enthralled with Simon, both in their attention and with their words. Scripture tells us that the people had been amazed by Simon for a long time. They were his followers. How much time did they give to something that was false and evil in nature?

The lesson here is not to be sucked in by every shiny new toy or awesome opportunity that presents itself. But to first, take the time to discern God's direction and involvement, to evaluate if a particular opportunity is useful, helpful or even a godly pursuit. We don't want to be hopping on board just because there is a lot of wow, wonder, and applause. And this can be drilled down even more into what we commit to, what we buy into, and how we spend our days. Kingdom living reminds us to be watchful of what opportunities and desires capture our attention and time.

This is something with which I greatly struggle. I can hear an idea or be asked to participate in something I know is an opportunity I would really enjoy or be able to bring value to the table. So, I say "Yes. Yes. And yes." But then eventually, I wind up being over-committed, which doesn't help anybody. Balancing my desires with my reality and current commitments is hard. It isn't that I can't say no, it is that *I don't want to say no*. Everything sounds fun and exciting until I find my attention and time pulled in too many ways. I must not have sought God for direction. Can anyone relate to this? We need to honestly examine our desires and our goals, and bring them before God in prayer. Sometimes, there will be desires and opportunities that are good, but it is not the right time. Seek God and be willing to yield.

> Kingdom living reminds us to be watchful of what opportunities and desires capture our attention and time.

�֎ **How are you doing with watching which opportunities and desires capture your time and attention? Is this an area for improvement?**

Day Three

One of my all-time favorite books is *A Man Called Peter*, the life story of Peter Marshall—a Scottish immigrant, born in 1902 who went on to become a pastor and the Chaplain of the U.S. Senate. He really has a great life story. He immigrated to the U.S. at the age of twenty-four with the call of God to enter the ministry. And God gave him favor, expanded his reach, and multiplied his audience (fairly sizably at times), but all the while, he remained humble.

At one of the churches Peter pastored, there was a young college girl, named Catherine, who became highly interested in this single pastor. She found herself thinking about him quite a bit and even wrote home about him. She had a pretty decent crush and yet, was deeply disappointed because she didn't think she would ever actually meet him. Eventually, a professor of hers scheduled both Peter and Catherine to speak at a prohibition rally, and they slowly got to know each other. Well, it is the sweetest love story of her hopes and desires rolled into what God wanted. Because once Peter realized and I mean *realized* that Catherine was God's plan for him, he wasted no time in proposing. And this is what Catherine said about the event:

> Yet he framed his proposal in gentle words, like the delicate embroidery surrounding the strong, simple words of an old sampler. I did not feel I could give him an immediate answer. We agreed to pray about it separately. Years before, Peter's life had been solemnly dedicated to his Chief. Both of us felt that the important thing now was to find out what God *wanted* for us. Were our paths to separate at this point, or was it possible that we together would be a greater asset to the Kingdom of God than we could ever be separately? My heart dictated the answer, but I was fearful that my heart might obscure God's mind on the matter.
>
> As unskilled and immature as I was in prayer, God chose this time to teach me a great lesson. I learned that just because God loves us so much, often He guides us by planting His own lovely dream in the barren soil of a human heart. When the dream has matured,

and the time for its fulfillment is ripe, to our astonishment and delight, we find that God's will has become our will, and our will, God's. Only God could have thought of a plan like that! [50]

Isn't that the best? Maybe you can sit here today and see how God planted a dream in your heart and how beautifully He worked it out. Or maybe you are sensing His wooing, and He is preparing the soil of your heart to receive a new desire. When our desires match God's desires, it is both to our astonishment and delight.

Have you experienced a time when God's will beautifully aligned with your own?

Why is it important that our desires don't clash with God's?

Despite Catherine's own desire to marry Peter, did you notice how she did not give her answer right away? Rather they agreed to pray about it separately.

I can remember being in college and hearing some of my friends say they wanted to homeschool their kids. And I can remember thinking, "Yikes, no way." And then as years continued to go by and I had children, I would think, "Lord, *please* do not call me to homeschool my children." It was not my desire whatsoever.

But as we faced various situations, the option appeared on the table. And over those next few months, the Lord planted the desire to homeschool in my heart. And as it took root, and grew and grew, I can tell you that I entered the season of homeschooling with joy and excitement, and feeling the pleasure of God. His desire for my kids' schooling had become my own, which just amazes me.

At times, we will enjoy our desires beautifully aligning with God's. But we also need to know that there will be times when we are called to lay aside our desires and submit to God's authority in our lives. How will we handle those times? Will we go kicking and screaming like the toddler not ready to go to bed? Or will we follow the Lord's leading because we know and trust His character?

Remember back to that summer job I took after college, the story I shared a couple of weeks ago? It wasn't the full-time youth ministry position I had wanted. But it meant following God's lead and submitting to His will—and it worked out better than I could have imagined. It meant laying aside my desire and surrendering to God's authority in my life.

How do you (or should you) handle the times when your desires don't align with God's?

Let's spend today's time in the Word looking up the following Scriptures. Take notes on what you need to remember from each passage and how it relates to aligning your dreams to God's desires.

Psalm 143:10

Proverbs 3:5-6

Proverbs 16:9

Luke 9:23-24

Jeremiah 17:7-8

In Acts 8, we saw that Simon's desires did not align with what God's will is for Kingdom living. I want you to think for a moment about the desires of your heart. Do they line up with God's desires for you? I hope you can say, "Yes." And if you don't know, then it is a matter for prayer.

> **Take a moment now to tune your heart to God's and make His desires for you a priority.**

Day Four

Well, with just two days left in this week, we had better pick up the pace. Today, we are going to look at Moses in Exodus 33. You may remember that we looked at this passage in our first week's video, but it is a perfect picture of what Moses most desired and what fueled those desires. Buckle up. We're heading back to the mountain with Moses.

Read Exodus 33:12-18. Record Moses' desires found in verses 13, 15, and 18.

Moses isn't shy about his requests, and I appreciate that about him. He wanted to learn God's ways. He desperately desired God's presence to go with him, and he wanted to see God's glory.

Remember, Moses had seen so much of God's glory already, but he still wanted more. I love that Moses asked for big things. On a TV show that my kids enjoy watching, the main character told her brother that if his dreams weren't scaring him, he wasn't dreaming big enough.[51] And while secularly, that is an interesting thought, as far as Kingdom living goes, we serve an amazing and all-powerful God who can do anything. We *can* dream big with Him!

What do you think fueled Moses' desire? Add your answers to the chart on page 100.

We are told in verse 13 that Moses wanted to learn God's ways so that he could know God better and find favor with Him. Moses desired companionship and closeness. I can't imagine what it would have been like to lead the Israelites out of Egypt and to lead them through the desert. I think God's presence for Moses was not only the opportunity to be close to the Lord Most High but also the nod of approval from God. It is hard to be a leader (especially when you've got 600,000 grumblers, whiners, and idolators—and that number doesn't count the women and children). God's presence was assurance to Moses that God was pleased with him, and it let everyone else know it as well.

So, what is it we learn from Moses and his desires in Exodus 33? First, we see that it is better to be *with* God in the desert than to be in the Promised Land *without* Him. Moses wanted God's presence to go with him or he didn't want to leave Sinai. Moses' desire for God to go with him should be our desire in any dream we possess. Why would we want to go somewhere that takes us outside of His presence? Have you ever wanted something but pursuing it took you outside of God's direction for your life? It will always be better to be living in His will then outside of His presence.

✣ **Can you share a time when you saw how it was better to be in the desert with God than in the 'Promised Land' without Him?**

We can also see that if our desire is to truly know God more, we can rest assured that like Moses our desire will always be met. What are you hungering for? Is it God?

I can think of times in my life when my spiritual walk was lacking. Times when I simply wasn't hungering for Him. Things were dry. It wasn't that I had given up on my faith, I just wasn't walking in intimacy and closeness with the Lord. And I can remember on a couple of occasions, just starting by asking Him, "Lord, give me a hunger for You." Such a simple prayer. "Give me a hunger." I would pray that for a while. And as if to see how much I really wanted it or how much I persisted, a couple of weeks would go by. Then all of a sudden, I would find I was hungering and thirsting for Him. I wanted to spend time with Him. It was food for my soul. And that is what I hope for each of us. That we would have that desire to be in His presence, to experience His glory, to speak to Him as if face to face. I love what a commentator said, ". . . Moses had to climb a mountain to meet with God. All you have to do is speak His Name."[52] An appetite for God is always met, but we need to be hungry!

What have been some of your sweetest times of being close with the Lord?

> It is better to be with God in the desert than to be in the Promised Land without Him.

> An appetite for God is always met, but we need to be hungry!

Moses wanted to know God's ways, to be in His presence, and to see His glory. And he got all three! Don't be afraid to dream big when it comes to knowing God.

Turn to Hebrews 11:6. What does this verse tell us about those who earnestly seek Him?

Yes! You can count on it! He rewards those who seek Him. Psalm 37:4 is a familiar verse, but it is sometimes taken out of context. The verse says, "Delight yourself in the LORD; And He will give you the desires of your heart" (NASB).[53] Some will look at this verse and just focus on the part that He will give us the desires of our heart. But we must look at the verse as a whole. "*Delight yourself in the LORD*; And He will give you the desires of your heart" (emphasis added). Does this mean He will give you any desire of your heart? No, that guarantee is not here. The key is that we are delighting ourselves in Him.

As we grow closer to Him and we *delight* in Him, I have to tell you, I think our desires change. Our perspectives change, our hopes change, our motives change. They become more in line with what God already wants for us and for our world.

You can also think of it this way: if we are delighting ourselves in Him and *He* is the desire of our heart, will He give us more of Himself? Every single time without a doubt!

And it just starts with a simple and persistent request.

✢ **How do you delight yourself in the Lord?**

Day Five

Our third and final individual to look at is David. Let's set the stage. This is a story you have likely heard before, but we are going to dig deeper into this account of a young shepherd boy and the giant. It is much more than a children's story where the underdog is victorious. What we see here has the ability to change the trajectory of our lives!

Remember the Philistines? Well, they are still at it with Israel. But now they have this great contender and his name is Goliath. He wore a bronze helmet and a coat of scale armor. And when it says scales, that is exactly what to picture in your mind. Think of the scales of a fish and how they overlap, one on top of another. This armor weighed 125lbs, so *crazy heavy*, right? Goliath also wore bronze grieves (armor) to protect his shins. He had a bronze javelin on his back and a spear with an iron point, which alone weighed 15lbs. For reference, my little dog weighs 10lbs! And Goliath was 9'9" tall and had someone in front of him to carry his shield. I think we can easily say he was very well protected.

This Philistine contender came out morning and night, shouting at the ranks of Israel to send someone out and fight him. In verse 10 of 1 Samuel 17, we see that one of the things Goliath shouted was "This day I defy the armies of Israel!" And Scripture tells us that Saul and the Israelites were dismayed and terrified. No one wanted to fight him.

Read 1 Samuel 17:20-29. Who does David argue with?

Doesn't this feel like a typical sibling conversation here between Eliab and David? David saw the usual banter of the Philistine and look at how he reacted. He was very concerned. But was his brother right? Was David just there for the thrill of watching the fight? Do you think he was interested only in what the victor received after killing the Philistine?

Keep something here in 1 Samuel and turn now to Acts 13:22. What was David called?

✣ **What does it mean to be called a person after God's own heart?**

We know from when David was called and anointed by Samuel (1 Samuel 16), God refused his older brothers but chose David because of his heart. It wasn't the tallest, the oldest, the biggest or the strongest that was to be anointed by Samuel—the ones who had the likely appearance of a future king. No, it was David, because as we learned earlier this week, God looks and cares about what is in the heart.

I read some beautiful commentaries that talked about the time David spent in the fields with sheep and how that time greatly grew his relationship with His Lord. If we know David was a man after God's own heart, it should be no surprise then to see what bothered David about Goliath's taunting. And the key is in the last sentence of verse 26 in 1 Samuel 17.

What did David say the "uncircumcised Philistine" was doing?

> *"Yes, LORD, walking in the way of your laws, we wait for you; your name and renown are the desire of our hearts."*
>
> —ISAIAH 26:8

To defy the armies of the living God was to defy the living God Himself. David was concerned for God's name, His reputation and His renown. Does that sound familiar? Renown is defined as "widespread and high repute; fame."[54] Reread Isaiah 26:8 in the margin.

According to 1 Samuel 17:26, what did David desire?

David wanted to defeat Goliath, the man who was defying the living God. He wanted to see the name and renown of God lifted up. Do we care about this as much as David?

Do you desire to see God's name lifted up and His renown increased?

Let's read 1 Samuel 17:30-40. What reason did Saul give to prevent David from fighting Goliath?

David responded to Saul with evidence that God had protected him in the past with the lion and the bear, and He will protect him again with the Philistine. Not only was David trusting God with his physical protection, he trusted Him with his desire. God was in control, and just as He was faithful in the past, He would be faithful in the future.

And that is true with us! We can trust God with the fruition of our dreams and desires. He is completely capable. Just as David entrusted his future to God, we can entrust our dreams and desires to our faithful King. (There are so many life applications here that I would love to hit, but we are just going to stay on task.)

Next, we see that David chose not to wear Saul's armor and instead went to the stream and picked up five stones. Why five stones? David knew full well that God could take care of Goliath with one stone. My research proved interesting here. One of the commentaries suggested that David selected five stones because Goliath had four brothers, and David was simply preparing for the possibility of

> Just as David entrusted his future to God, we can entrust our dreams and desires to our faithful King.

them coming out to avenge his death.[55] It is a fascinating thought, but we don't know for sure.

David picked up the stones, put them in his shepherd's pouch, and grabbed his staff and sling shot. That is it. Can you imagine the scene? I mean my husband, Dan, is nearly 6'6", so add another three feet—three inches and you would have Goliath. And here comes this teenage, shepherd boy with his staff and a sling shot. A sling shot with which he probably had much practice over the years in those fields. And that was all he needed.

God will always equip us with whatever we need to face the giant in our own lives. If there is something standing in the way of our heart's desire (and I mean those that align with His—please don't miss that), He will equip us with exactly what we need to find victory. David didn't need Saul's armor. He needed only the stones and the sling shot.

Let's pick up in verse 41 and read through 47. What was Goliath's response to the shepherd boy?

God will always equip us with whatever we need to face the giant in our own lives.

I love this. David told Goliath, "You come to me with a sword and with a spear and with a javelin, but I come to you in the name of the LORD of hosts, the God of the armies of Israel, whom you have defied" (1 Samuel 17:45, ESV).[56] This "LORD of hosts" is the Hebrew name for God, Yahweh Tsabaot (tsaw-baw-Oth) or the Greek version, Jehovah Sabaoth.

And I love that David used this name here. Jehovah Sabaoth is used 260 times in the Old Testament and "saba" means "a mass [as in a lot] of people or things, especially for war, a campaign, an army." And Sabaoth commonly has a military connotation.[57] Picture this teenage shepherd with his sling shot and staff, running up alone, void of any other men standing with him in support. What does he tell Goliath? Read it once more. "You come to me with a sword and with a spear and with a javelin, but I come to you in the name of the LORD of hosts, the God of the armies of Israel, whom you have defied."[58]

David has the Lord of Hosts, the God of Israel's armies, and leader of a mass number of heavenly soldiers ready and waiting with him. You see, when we are fighting for something in God's plan for our lives, we can know He shows up, ready for battle. And the battle truly is His! There is no stopping Him!

> **Notice with me that right here in David's speech, we can see what fueled his desire. Look at the end of verse 46. Why does David want to beat Goliath?**

Wow! That is fuel for the fire. As your dreams and desires are fulfilled, will the world look at your life and see there is a God in your life? Will the desires of your heart bring glory to God? Will His name be lifted up and exalted in your life? Will He be the ultimate desire of your heart?

> **Take a moment and write a prayer asking God to make you a woman after His own heart.**

Time to wrap up this week! Complete the chart on the next page and I'll see you in the video.

Fuel for the Fire

Complete this chart as you study our three individuals and their desires.

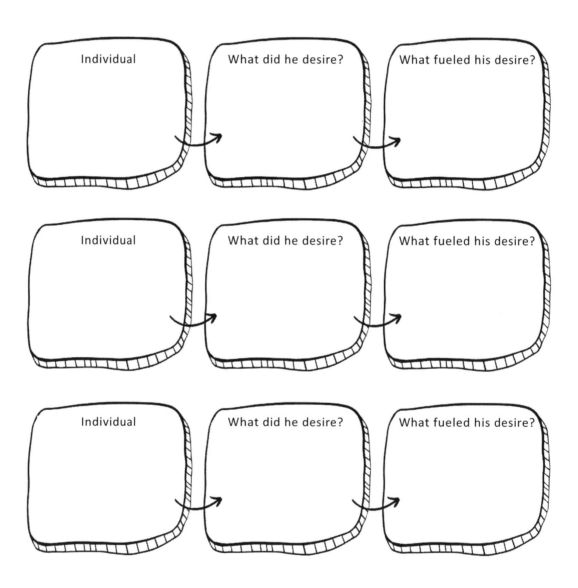

Individual	What did he desire?	What fueled his desire?

Fuel for the Fire

Money did not fuel Robert A. Jaffray's desire, _____ did.

Genesis 15:1

God tells Abram not to _____.

The Lord calls Abram by _____.

God assures Abram that He is his _____.

God is not just the rewarder, He is also the _____.

When we think of all the desires of our hearts, they all _____ in comparison to Him.

Video lessons are available at KristenTiber.com/GreaterGloryVideos.

Week Five
Present Sufferings

"And the God of all grace,
who called you to his eternal glory in Christ,
after you have suffered a little while,
will himself restore you and make you
strong, firm and steadfast.
To him be the power for ever and ever.
Amen."

1 PETER 5:10-11

Day One

How is it that we are starting our final week together? I am so thankful for you and for this opportunity to grow deeper in our faith and knowledge of God. I have enjoyed studying the glory of God with you so much.

But I have to confess that of all of the weeks of looking at God's glory, this fifth week has been the most intimidating to me. And that is because we are looking at the snapshot of suffering and how through our suffering, we can bring God glory. As I think of those going through this study, I know there are individuals who have and are facing great challenges: life and death issues, health problems, intense family struggles . . . all sorts of things. And while I have gone through some very difficult times in my life, I can easily look around and see so many who are suffering much more than I ever have. So it is for that reason I feel intimidated to have any word on the matter.

But thankfully, we are not here for what I have to say. Truly, our hope and help come from God alone. So this week, as we usually do, we are going to once again turn to the Word of God to see what it is He has to say.

First though, I would like to clarify that there are many kinds of suffering. It is my intent not to exclude anything. As we talk of suffering, I would like you to think of the trivial suffering of things going wrong on a particular day (your kids being sick or your car getting a flat tire), all the way to the toughest experiences of terminal illness or the loss of a child—because God is there for all of it.

Elisabeth Elliott gave what I consider a simple, but excellent definition of suffering, and it is this: "Suffering is having what you do not want or wanting what you do not have."[59]

✤ What do you think of this definition? Is it accurate?

❖ **Write a few examples below.**

This definition is able to cover it all, from the small things that we do not want like a sprained ankle to the big things like cancer. From desiring to be free of physical pain or wanting a roof that doesn't leak to longing for an easy family life. From parenting a young, challenging child through the season of learning obedience to handling a teen who is making poor choices. Each can be a season of suffering.

And the reason I would like you to consider all sorts of suffering as we work through this lesson is because life is hard. No one gets through this life without suffering at some capacity. Bad things happen. Whether it is a result of sin, the fallen world in which we live or because our battle is not against flesh and blood, but principalities and powers of evil (Ephesians 6:12), we will each experience difficult things and challenging times. And the Bible deals with suffering head-on. There are even times when the Apostle Paul makes suffering sound like a rite of passage.

> No one gets through this life without suffering at some capacity.

Are you in a season of suffering? What are you suffering through right now, big or small?

There are so many places we could go in the Scriptures, but this week, we are going to set up camp in John 11, the story of Lazarus and his sisters.

Please read John 11:1-3. What was wrong with Lazarus?

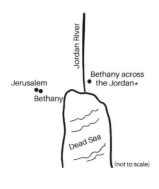

*This map shows
the traditional site of
"the Bethany across the Jordan."
Some scholars think that it could
be farther north.

From which village is Lazarus from?

I want to make sure you understand the location of where things are happening here in our text. There are two cities named Bethany in the New Testament. One is just two miles east of Jerusalem on the slope of the Mount of Olives, and the other is farther east across the Jordan River. The second one is characterized as just that—"the Bethany across the Jordan."[60] Our Bethany, here in John 11, is the first one—the village near Jerusalem where Lazarus lived.

And if we look back to verse 40 of John 10, we see that Jesus, having left Jerusalem, headed even further east. He went across the Jordan River to where John had been baptizing (the other Bethany) because the Jews were trying to seize him. So as we start John 11, it is helpful to know that Jesus is in Bethany *on the other side* of the Jordan River, twenty miles away when he learns Lazarus is ill.[61]

Another important thing to note is John's purpose in writing his Gospel. Turn to John 20:30-31. What two reasons did John give for writing about what Jesus did?

Belief and life. In John 10:10, we read that Jesus came that we may have life and have life more abundantly. Was Jesus telling us that we will not suffer then? Was He teaching that when we are found in Him, there is a removal of all suffering? No. He knew we would suffer. But abundant life can still be ours in the hard times because of Him!

We will see this in the most literal sense this week. As readers who likely know the end of this story, to what was Lazarus restored? To life. And that life is given in Jesus' name, and we will see that many who witnessed this miracle came to believe in Jesus. Belief and life.

But let's not get too far ahead. Lazarus is sick. He is suffering. The illness is very serious if death is indeed on the doorstep. So Mary and Martha sent word to

Jesus. And as probably everyone reading this has experienced and can attest, the suffering of one person isn't felt by the individual alone, but also by those who love him or her. The pain we can feel when we know and love someone who is going through a physical, mental or emotional crisis situation can bring suffering into our own lives. Now please know that I am not saying this is a bad thing, because truly it is evidence of our love for that person. But when those we love suffer, we suffer with them in our heart.

How did Mary and Martha characterize Lazarus to Jesus in John 11:3?

Mary and Martha, suffering on behalf of their brother, sent word that Lazarus, or as they put it—the one that Jesus loves—was sick. Why is this significant? Because in the midst of our suffering, we need to remember that we are loved by Jesus.

Our suffering did not start because God stopped loving us. The hardships we encounter are not a result of the lack of the Father's love. There are many reasons we may experience something difficult. And at times, we may not even know why we are facing a given situation.

Now, can some of our suffering be a direct result of what we have done? Yes. Sure it can! Our own sin can have great effects, and as we know from studying 1 Samuel 4, God *will* allow hardships at times because of our disobedience. He may use that suffering to bring us back into fellowship with Him. But suffering is not *always* because of this.

Think back to our look at Job. Was Job's suffering because he had sinned? No, it was as a result of Satan's challenge. How about Joseph? Did he suffer because he had done something wrong? No, it was because of the sinful nature of his brothers, the lie of Potiphar's wife, and the forgetfulness of the cupbearer. There is no reason here to think that Lazarus' suffering was a result of his sin. It could simply have been that in a fallen world, we experience pain and sickness.

> In the midst of our suffering, we need to remember that we are loved by Jesus.

Whatever the cause of our own suffering though, we can know that God still loves us. If our suffering is a means of discipline, He is doing what is for our best, out of His love, to bring us back to Him. But at other times, it may just be a matter of life being hard, of sin being in the world, or an attack from the enemy. Yet, we need to remember that in the midst of our hardships and trials, His love is still there!

Read Psalm 136:1 and write it below.

If you are sitting here this week and feeling the strain of suffering, does it help to remember that you are loved by the Most High? He considers you His child, His daughter, the apple of His eye. If you were the only human being alive, the Father still would have sent His Son to pay the penalty for your sin with His death on the cross. Yes, you are loved!

And because He loves us, we can bring anything to Him at all! Any heartache. Any prayer. Any request. Just as Mary and Martha did.

✦What request do you want to bring before Him right now?

Day Two

Let's start by reading John 11:4-10. What did Jesus do when He learned that Lazarus was sick (according to verse 6)?

It may appear, at quick glance, that Jesus doesn't care about Lazarus because he chose to stay two more days across the Jordan River after hearing from Mary and Martha. But that couldn't be further from the truth.

What do we see confirmed in verse 5?

We should never interpret God's delay in our suffering as His disinterest. We see right here in Scripture that Jesus loved not only Lazarus, but also Mary and Martha. His delay was not due to indifference.

About six years ago, Dan and I began the process of building what would be our dream house. We had sold our house, moved our family into my mom's home and started the process of designing and making all the fun selections that go with building your own house. We were one week away from breaking ground when my husband received news that his job security was . . . well, not secure. The company had been bought and was undergoing changes. His job in particular was at risk, and all of a sudden, we were facing the possibility of him losing his job when we were about to take on a giant financial responsibility.

Our builder was a friend, and I knew he started his day at the crack of dawn, so I texted him very early the next morning. And at 6:30 a.m., he called me back, and I explained our situation. He couldn't have been more gracious about delaying the project. But that didn't help my heartache and sadness.

I was not only concerned for Dan, for what he was going through, the stress of the situation, and what job loss could mean for our family, but also sad at the fact that we couldn't build the new house. We don't take financial risks or gambles. We purposely didn't even begin building until we sold the last house because we didn't want the potential stress of two mortgages. So obviously, building was off until one of two things happened: Dan regained his job security or he found a new job (which would require reassessment to ensure we could afford the project).

To tell you I was disappointed about not building the house I had worked so hard on is an understatement. I could not even drive by our new street. I purposely drove a different route when taking my kids to school because seeing the street where our house was supposed to be built was just too sad.

It took about three weeks before I could drive by the street without tearing up. But finally, I arrived at the place where I could say, "Lord, if that is not your will for us . . . so be it." So be it. I could finally say I wanted His will more than my own and if I never built our house, it would be okay with me. So we waited on Him. Waited to see what He would do. How He would move. And it took a while.

His delay in bringing resolution to our situation, however, was not because He was disinterested in what was going on in our lives. On the contrary, He was working with love to draw us closer to Him—to a greater place of surrender and trust. There was purpose. His purpose.

❖ **Can you think of a time when you had to wait for "resolution" to your suffering? Did you find it hard to wait? Why or why not?**

❖ **How did God show Himself to be faithful in your situation?**

In the end, God brought resolution, and we were able to build our house. But even more amazing was the way He strengthened our faith and gave purpose to that time. Here, in what we just read, Jesus revealed the bottom line—the purpose—of what the account in John 11 was all about and why the situation was moving in that particular direction.

Read verse 4 again. Record the purpose Jesus gave.

Whenever we see the Son glorified, God the Father is glorified, and the opposite is true as well. I was surprised to see how often in the New Testament as I was looking at two of the most predominant Greek words for glory that they were tied to suffering. It was crazy. Most often, I found it connected to Jesus' suffering and glory. But there were also many verses that tied *our* suffering to glory as well.

Turn to Romans 8:16-18. What two things does Scripture relate together?

Oh man, I love this. When I think of the suffering that we face (that many of us currently face), doesn't it sound good that in all this suffering, God has glory on His mind? And if we share in His sufferings, we will share in His glory! Even trying to live a godly lifestyle will bring suffering in this life. But the hope is that we will share in His glory.

Savor the encouragement given in verse 18 about our present sufferings (whether persecution as a believer, watching bad things happen because we live in a fallen and dying world or simply feeling the effects of sin in our day-in and day-out life). I am so glad to know that these "present sufferings" aren't even worth comparing to the glory that will be revealed in us. Isn't that good to hear today? Hang in there in your suffering. Glory is coming.

And while it is revealed in us, who's glory is it ultimately?

_____

How does the future glory compare to your present sufferings?

We can find comfort by viewing our present sufferings in light of the future glory to be revealed.

Jesus waited two days, and then He told His disciples that they were going back to Judea. But the disciples were surprised. Why? Remember back to the fact that the Jewish leaders were trying to seize Jesus. The leaders wanted to stone Him as recorded in the previous chapter. But Jesus' response demonstrates His confidence in God's providence.

Just as there is a set time of daylight each day and no one will change that, if the Father has given the Son work to do, it will happen, and no one will interfere with that plan.[62] God is most certainly in control. In John 9:4, Jesus said that as long as it is still day, He must do the works of the One who sent Him. He reminded his disciples "that He was on the Father's schedule, and that nothing could harm them."[63]

As we face times of suffering, we need to remember that God is still on the throne. We are on His schedule. Nothing happens outside of what He allows. And I realize that could be hard for some of you to hear—that He has allowed your suffering to happen. But if we believe God is in control then yes, He allows bad things to happen due to the fact that He has given us free will, this is a sinful world, and we have an enemy who is still roaming. But I find comfort that our God is still on the throne, and He is in control. And we know His character. We trust His heart and we find confidence in His purpose.

How does the fact that God is in control bring you comfort?

Day Three

During the summer of the COVID-19 pandemic, I placed an order for beginner bras from Target.com for my daughter. When the 3-pack of undergarments arrived, it was clear I had ordered the wrong size, and they would need to be exchanged. After spending the morning on the beach of Lake Erie, my family was near a Target store, so I ran in to return the bras. I hoped I could do this quickly because my family was waiting in the car.

At customer service, an employee greeted me and asked how she could help. I told her I had a return and placed the folded bras in their clear plastic bag on the counter. She proceeded to tell me that she couldn't accept the return. I assumed it was that they were not accepting returns as some stores had adopted that policy during a portion of the pandemic. (Although all the stores I knew had lifted that policy by this point.) I asked when I would be able to make the return to which she responded, "Never. These cannot be returned."

I politely informed her that nowhere on the item's webpage did it say that, nor in the email with the barcode to help process returns. She said (and with a motion of her hand from head to neck), "Because they are near your face, Target cannot accept the return."

I must have said, "I don't understand," numerous times. And as we were making no progress and my level of frustration was increasing, I asked to speak with a manager. I didn't get it. Why was this not a simple process? She again made the motion brushing by her face, which I could only interpret as the bra having to go over your face when trying it on. But I still didn't understand. When did bras become ineligible for returns?

And then it dawned on me. This was one big misunderstanding.

As I realized what she thought these sweet beginner bras were, I exclaimed, "These are training bras!" She responded with a sigh of relief. This whole time, she had thought they were face masks! And when you looked at them through the plastic, I could see how she might have thought that. Albeit the cute little bow on the top "mask" was something, she confessed, she had not seen before.

We had a good laugh. She apologized, and I told her I now understood everything she was saying. We parted with giggles, and I'm sure the Target break room had a good chuckle over the misunderstanding.

Read John 11:11-16. What did the disciples misunderstand in regard to what Jesus told them about Lazarus?

The disciples did not grasp the meaning of what Jesus was saying. And because the disciples misunderstood, Jesus had to plainly tell them that Lazarus had died.

You know looking at Thomas here, we often fault him for his lack of faith, but we cannot fault him for his loyalty. He was expecting that a visit to Bethany, being just two miles from Jerusalem, would draw the Jewish leaders and renew the threats and attempts on Jesus' life and quite possibly, on the lives of the disciples as well. Yet, he maintained his allegiance. His thinking was along the lines of: *By all means, we (disciples and Jesus) will die too, along with Lazarus.*

In verse 15, what was Jesus glad about?

Notice that Jesus did not say that He was glad Lazarus had died. Rather He said that He was glad He wasn't there for the sake of His disciples. But only we, knowing the full story, understand the reason. Because truly, what they were about to witness was going to be one of the most climactic miracles of Jesus' ministry.

Read John 11:17-27.

Which sister went to meet Jesus when she learned of His coming?

_____

What did she say to Jesus?

When Jesus arrived, Lazarus had already been in the tomb for four days. Martha was confident that had Jesus been there, her brother would have been healed. Why? Because she knew Jesus. She knew what He was like and what He could do. At the end of the book of John, John tells us that Jesus did many other things and if every one of them had been written down, that he supposed even the whole world would not have enough room for the books that would be written (John 21:25). So keep in mind, what we have here in the Gospels is a sampling of everything that Jesus did. It gives us enough to _know and believe,_ but there was much more. More miracles, more healings, and as one scholar suggested, probably more raisings from the dead than the three we have in the Gospels.[64]

Martha then acknowledged that even now God the Father would give Jesus whatever He asked. And Jesus told her that Lazarus would rise again. However, she misinterpreted this for the final resurrection at the end of days. Whereas, Jesus had something much more immediate in mind.

✢ **Pay particularly close attention to Jesus' response in verse 25. How did He identify Himself?**

This is the fifth of seven "I AM" statements that John records in his Gospel. In the Greek, these "I AM" statements clearly allude to the self-disclosure of God's name, "I AM," found in Exodus 3 during the encounter of Moses and the burning bush.[65]

Record the seven identifications found in John's Gospel.

- John 6:35 _____

- John 9:5 _____

- John 10:7 _____

- John 10:11 _____

- John 11:25 I am the resurrection and the life. _____

- John 14:6 _____

- John 15:1 _____

What I love is that God, in each of the instances, reveals more about Himself related to the given situation. Even in the Old Testament, we can look at the times when God revealed Himself by a new name and how it connected to the situation at hand. Examples include: Yahweh Tsabaoth—the Lord of Hosts (as we saw last week); Jehovah Nissi—the Lord our Banner; Yahweh Shalom—the Lord our peace; El Shaddai—Lord Almighty all sufficient; Jehovah Tsidkenu—the Lord our righteousness; El Elyon—the Lord Most High; Jehovah Rapha—the Lord that heals you. Every time our Lord revealed more and more about Himself with each name or identifier.

Here we see Lazarus in the grave. Dead and buried. The stone rolled in front; the tomb closed up. And Jesus said, "I am the resurrection and the life." Lazarus was facing the final enemy of death, and Jesus takes it right back and says *He* is the resurrection and the life. He takes where we are, in whatever situation we may be and reveals Himself. And doesn't He still do that today?

After my dad left when I was 15, it was a rough couple of years. My mom had not wanted the divorce, and during that time, she went through clinical depression. When she would be really upset over something, I would pick up the phone and call one of three particular friends and ask them to talk to her. At that age, I really didn't know what else to do to help other than pray. Well one day, my mom told me NOT to call her friends anymore. And being the obedient daughter, I wasn't going to.

But one of those horrible days came, and I remember hearing my mom outside "doing yard work"—you know, the kind of yard work you do when you're angry or upset about something. I was upstairs in my room, and I just prayed, "Lord, since I'm not allowed to call someone, please have one of her friends call us."

The phone didn't ring.

But within five minutes, I heard a car pull in the drive. It was one of my mom's friends. She stepped out of the car and told my mom that she was driving down the street, and the Lord told her to come over. Wow!

In that moment, I knew He hears our requests, He responds to our cries, and He is present in our sufferings. He doesn't go into hiding. And if I had ever doubted whether God was with us in our situation at that time, all doubt was gone with the sound of that friend's car pulling in the driveway because God was there with me, hearing my every request. He was present. He revealed to me personally that He was Immanuel, God with us.

Martha talks about the future resurrection as a doctrine. But as one commentator made note, "Jesus states it as *a fact*, identified with His own person. He does not say, *I raise the dead*; I *perform* the resurrection, but I *am* the resurrection."[66]

We can ask God to reveal more about who He is in every situation we face. Whatever ails us, He doesn't just perform the fix or the healing, He is the fix and the healing. If we are anxious, He doesn't just give us peace, He is peace. If we are confused about what is true, He is the truth. When we are broken-hearted, He is the mender. When we feel like we are in the dark, He is the light. When we are tired, He is our rest. When we are weak, He is our strength. When we feel like we can no longer bear what we are going through and live, He is life.

✢ **What has the Lord revealed to you about Himself in times of suffering?**

Day Four

There is something about suffering that causes some to question their beliefs, some to come to faith, and others to solidify what it is that they believe. I have a friend who fought cancer, and what her friends and family witnessed was an incredible deepening of her faith in God during that time. She dug her feet down deep into the truth of His Word and stood strong. And even today, after years in remission, she still shares of His goodness and mercy.

Yesterday, we saw that Jesus declared to Martha's heart that He was the resurrection and the life. Those who believed in Him would never die. And Jesus asked Martha if she believed it.

Reread John 11:27. What is it that Martha said she believed?

In the midst of her suffering, Martha offered this beautiful confession of faith in who Jesus is—He is the Messiah (the Anointed One), the Son of God, who has come into the world.

Martha *believes*. And right there, Martha has a real victory. You see, we have an enemy who wants to destroy our faith. The Word tells us that Satan comes to steal, kill, and destroy (John 10:10), and he is after your faith. I mentioned earlier about my mom and her friend. This friend also told my mom that Satan wasn't after her marriage. He was after her faith.

What is it that you are going through and need to realize that Satan is after your faith? He wants to beat you up and wear you down until you start questioning and doubting. To shoot those fiery darts of Ephesians 6 into your shield of faith. Maybe it is something big or maybe he is using all the little things put together. But know this, he doesn't want you to walk in victory. He wants your faith!

Beth Moore, in one of her Sunday School classes (available as a podcast), was teaching on Ephesians 6, the armor of God.[67] In the teaching, she shared about the shield of faith and the fiery darts of the enemy. Beth shared a story that she had found about the Roman centurion, Sceva, who fought under Caesar's command. After an enormous battle, the heads of the army on the field wanted Caesar to know and realize how much courage the soldiers had shown and to know the intensity of the battle fought. So they gathered the soldiers' shields, pulled the darts out of each one, and laid them before Caesar. Sceva had 220 darts in his shield! Think about that for a moment. Two hundred and twenty darts in one man's shield. Caesar was so astonished that he rewarded the soldiers with a double portion of pay, gifts, and promotions.

Following the story, Beth Moore made the point that we think we don't want the darts. We don't want the battle (those periods of suffering). We want God to remove everything that is hard in our lives. But if that is what we want, we are working against what it is that He wants for us. Instead of having every hard thing removed, the Father wants to see us choose to believe Him in the midst of the battle, to hold up that shield of faith. The point isn't that at the end, we have made it through without darts in our shield. The point is that we do have the darts. And we present them before our Commander and Chief as she put it. Why?

The answer is found in Hebrews 11:6. Look again at this verse and summarize it below.

Read the *New King James Version* of Hebrews 11:6. "But without faith it is impossible to please Him, for he who comes to God must believe that He is, and that He is a rewarder of those who diligently seek Him."[68] Our faith pleases

God. Holding up that shield of faith pleases God. We honor Him when we pull out all those darts that we face in our lives and present them to Him as a sacrifice. Hold up your shield of faith, sister in Christ.

How many darts do you have flying at you right now? How do you handle them? *You believe*. You stretch that faith muscle remembering that God is pleased when we exercise our faith in the midst of our suffering.

Martha goes back and calls her sister aside. She does this secretly. Do you wonder why? Most likely, they too believed that it wasn't safe for Jesus to be there, and we have read that many had come from Jerusalem to share in their grief.

Our faith in
the midst of
our suffering
pleases God.

Read John 11:28-31. How does Mary respond when she heard that the Teacher was asking for her?

The teacher was asking for her. This word "teacher" or "master" in verse 28—the Greek word didaskalos (did-as'-kal-os)—can mean teacher, master[69] or instructor—someone acknowledged for their mastery in their field of learning.[70] Jesus, as the Son of God, wins the prize for mastery in every field of learning. Geology, philosophy, chemistry, psychology, and so on—He created them all. He is the Master Teacher.

And this is the lesson for us: If the Teacher arrives, there is something to be learned.

If the Teacher arrives,
there is something to
be learned.

When we are in the midst of suffering and the Teacher arrives (and we know He does), there is something to be learned. What is God teaching us through our suffering? Is it reliance on Him? Is it to find our peace outside of our circumstance? Is it to find our strength in Him? Or our focus, our joy, our excitement for life? What is He teaching us in our suffering? Each experience may teach many things and be unique to each person. But have no doubt that God wants to teach us. We are to grow in our faith when we face any trial or hardship, whether it is a rough day, a rough four days or a rough four years.

After my dad left, someone told my mom that she envied what my mom was about to go through with the Lord during that incredible time of trial. That may sound backwards, but the Lord was about to teach my mom so much. And for me as well, it was an unparalleled time of growing and learning.

> **What a waste it would be not to learn what God wants to teach us. What have you learned through your times of suffering?**

Day Five

Let's not waste time. Are you as excited as I am to see every last detail of our story?

> **Read John 11:32-37. What position did Mary put herself in before Jesus?**

> **Why is this significant?**

Mary is humbling herself before the Lord. Does that make you think back to Ezekiel in chapter 3 or to the people in Leviticus 9 whom we talked about in the first week?

Turn back to page 19. What did Ezekiel do when he saw the glory of God?

Whether in times of glory or times of suffering, our proper position is always one of humility. How do we assert ourselves before God? We need a humble heart.

Are you able to maintain a humble heart in times of suffering?

Mary took Jesus to the tomb, and we see that He wept. I am incredibly thankful that we have a high priest, who according to Hebrews 4:15, is able to empathize with our weakness. In His tears, Jesus reveals His humanity and the fact that He "entered into all of our experiences and knows how we feel."[71]

Those around Him saw the evidence of Jesus' love in His tears.[72] We don't serve a stoic God who threw the cosmos into being and then sat back to watch how it all plays out from a distance. Rather, He is intimately involved in the lives and stories of His people. Aren't you grateful? We can rest in the fact that our Heavenly Father is intimately involved in our lives, and empathizes with us in our suffering.

Let's get to the whole glory part, alright?

Read John 11:38-44. What was Martha concerned about when Jesus instructed for the stone to be taken away?

> Whether in times of glory or times of suffering, our proper position is always one of humility.

> We can rest in the fact that our Heavenly Father is intimately involved in our lives, and empathizes with us in our suffering.

According to Jewish superstition at that time, the soul did not depart the body until the third day.[73] So for Jesus to wait until the fourth day to raise Lazarus completely obliterated any thought that the spirit of Lazarus was still there.

And Martha was so practical; you've gotta love her! She was worried about the smell. I am pretty sure, however, if the Savior calls you, the stink of death will be gone.

I love what Jesus said here, "Did I not tell you that if you believe, you will see the glory of God?" We do not need to doubt that God will show up and show us His glory. He will show up! It may not be with clouds and pillars of fire, but He will show up!

They rolled away the stone, and Jesus looked up to pray. Oh how I would have loved a view of the heavenlies as the Son looked up to the Father to pray. He prayed aloud for the benefit of those listening. He wanted them to *know* and *believe* that He had been sent by the Father, that what He was about to do was the will of the Father, and that the Father would get the glory.[74] He thanked His Father for hearing Him, for always hearing Him. And then in a loud voice, he called Lazarus out. I have heard on a couple of occasions, that had Jesus not specifically named Lazarus, the whole cemetery might have emptied out! Can you imagine what a sight that would have been?

Lazarus came out, grave clothes and all. And Jesus told the people to take off the cloth and let him go. So Lazarus was delivered. He was free. The suffering of Mary and Martha had ended. Lazarus had been raised and was free to go and live.

I once heard a fantastic teaching in Beth Moore's Bible study on Daniel[75] about God's deliverance in regard to Shadrach, Meshach and Abednego when Nebuchadnezzar was going to throw them into the blazing furnace for not bowing down to the gold statue. The three young Hebrew men responded in Daniel 3:16-18, "King Nebuchadnezzar, we do not need to defend ourselves before you in this matter. If we are thrown into the blazing furnace, the God we serve is able to deliver us from it, and he will deliver us from Your Majesty's hand. But even if he does not, we want you to know, Your Majesty, that we will not serve your gods or worship the image of gold you have set up."

Her teaching was that God will always deliver us, and it is in one of three ways.

- **He will deliver us <u>from</u> the fire.**[76] As in we won't have to go into the fire. The fire or situation is removed from our path before we have to enter it. I think about the mammogram and ultrasound I shared about in our introduction video—it didn't end up being anything. I was delivered from going into the fire.

- **He will deliver us <u>through</u> the fire.**[77] And this is what happened to Shadrach, Meshach and Abednego. They went into the fire, but the Lord rescued them through it, and they came out unharmed. This is when we have to suffer through something, but we come out of it by God's hand.

- **He will deliver us <u>by</u> the fire** and into His eternal arms.[78] The fire will be the means by which He brings us home to Him, for all eternity.

> In one way or another, God delivers us from our suffering.

I have been reading a book by John Piper in which he looks at God's passion for His glory and living the vision of Jonathan Edwards. One thing John Piper shared that has really stuck in my mind is that God is glorified when death is gain.[79] And this is most certainly something we know as believers in that Paul says to be absent from the body is to be present with the Lord (2 Corinthians 5:8), and to live is Christ and to die is gain (Philippians 1:20-21).

We certainly know that. But to live it, to fully comprehend that God gets glory when we see death for the believer as great gain, is an amazing thought. John Piper goes on to say, "The reason for this is plain: the glory of Christ is magnified when our hearts are more satisfied in him than in all that death takes from us. If we count death gain, because it brings us closer to Christ (which is what Philippians 1:23 says it does), then we show that Christ is more to be desired than all this world can offer."[80] Wow!

Jesus told the people to let Lazarus go. And if we look at it rightly, Lazarus was only suffering while he was sick. Death had freed him from his suffering. But Mary, Martha, and their friends were suffering in their sadness and grief. Their turmoil was ongoing. But Jesus came to meet the need, to be the answer, and to bring comfort as only He could.

There was a little girl about seven years old, and she went with her mother to a healing service. Now before I lose you, this wasn't some crazy healing service with all the fanfare. It was probably about twenty people praying for each other in a half-lit sanctuary one evening. But the purpose was to pray for healing, for relief from suffering. That little girl's mother was up front with the others, and the girl sat in the wooden pew of this very large, dimly-lit church. As she looked up, she saw a pink cloud hovering in the ceiling of the sanctuary. No one else seemed to be seeing it. At one point, it started to descend, slowly and peacefully. And in the words that a seven-year old would use, she later told her mom that when the cloud touched her, she felt "a twinkle in her heart."

This is a story that outside of a small group of people has never been shared. But 35 years later, after seeing that "pink cloud" with my own eyes, that Shekinah glory in that sense, I am for the first time asking the Lord why there. Why did the glory show up there? And the only answer I keep coming back to is that people were suffering.

People were suffering.

And God's glory is intimately connected to our suffering in a way I think I've only begun to understand. Consider the suffering Jesus went through on the cross, what was accomplished through that suffering (the redemption of His people), and the glory that followed. Elisabeth Elliott described the connection between suffering and glory in this way: "the cross [meaning suffering] is the gateway to joy" and participating in God's glory. In suffering, we taste the afflictions of the Son.[81]

What do you think she means?

How does seeing our sufferings with a "greater glory for God" mindset change our ability to endure?

The mindset of *greater glory* gives value to our suffering, the depths of which I had never thought before. Read 2 Corinthians 4:17 in the Amplified version. "For our momentary, light distress [this passing trouble] is producing for us an eternal weight of glory [a fullness] beyond all measure [surpassing all comparisons, a transcendent splendor and an endless blessedness]!"[82]

I am greatly encouraged to think of one day laying aside my present sufferings for an endless measure of glory that will go on forever—or as Paul David Tripp put it, "the never-ending ocean that is the glory of God."[83]

Will you live with a "greater glory" mindset? Will you allow God to use your suffering to bring Him glory? I wish I could hear your answers. For now, write *yes* or *no* in the blank below.

Will you allow God to use your suffering to bring Him glory?
_____.

Of all the things we have learned about suffering this week, what is most speaking to you?

See you in our last video!

VIDEO NOTES: WEEK 5

Present Sufferings

In all our suffering, we need to remember that this world is not our _____.

Remembering our _____ in Christ can serve as a great comfort in the midst of trials and hardships.

Our circumstance does not define His grace nor our _____.

We have a _____ hope based not on our own situation, but on the person of Jesus and His resurrection from the dead.

An eternal _____ reminds us of the inheritance and future glory that will one day be ours.

There is nothing quite like _____ to refine our faith.

A refined faith brings praise, _____, and honor to Jesus.

Video lessons are available at KristenTiber.com/GreaterGloryVideos.

ABOUT THE AUTHOR

Kristen Tiber

Kristen Tiber is an author, speaker, and women's Bible study teacher. Currently, she and her husband, Dan, teach the high school Sunday school class at their church and have enjoyed doing so for the last eight years. Kristen is a homeschooling mom to her two kids, Peter and Anna. A forever student of the Word of God, Kristen desires to see Jesus' name and renown lifted up. She is passionate to see others grow in their love for Jesus and His Word. Her books include *Teach Me To Serve* and *At The Well*. Kristen can be found at KristenTiber.com, where she encourages others to live with purpose in all seasons of life.

WOULD YOU LIKE FIVE PRINTABLE SCRIPTURE VERSES TO MEMORIZE ABOUT GOD'S GLORY?

Visit the *Greater Glory* video page
and scroll to the bottom to download the free printables.

WERE YOU BLESSED BY THIS BIBLE STUDY?

*Please consider leaving a review on Amazon or Goodreads
to help us reach others with the message of* Greater Glory.

How to Have a
Personal Relationship With Jesus

You may have heard people talk about having a personal relationship with God, and maybe that has left you with some questions. *Can I really know God? Does He know me? What does it mean to have a personal relationship when I can't see the One I'm supposed to be getting to know? How do you know if you're in a relationship with God? And what difference does it even make?*

Well first, let's take a couple of steps back. As you have most likely read in the first day of our study, creation reveals the glory of God. Creation also points to the fact that there is a Creator. When we look out our window and see the beauty, the design, the detail, and complexity of all of creation, we see the evidence of a masterful Creator. All of this did not come from nothing. Someone had to create it. Just like this book didn't pop into existence, but rather someone wrote it, someone printed it, and someone made sure it got to you—the same is true with creation. The complex design of the human body alone points us to the reality of forethought and a meticulous Designer.

So in order to talk about relationship, we have to first acknowledge that there is a God. In the Bible (the inspired and authoritative Word of God given to us), we learn about Him. We learn about His character, His deeds, and His love for us.

But there is a problem.

You see, we (you and I) have a sin problem. We do sinful things. We think unholy thoughts. We can be selfish and prideful. And in all this, we sin against our Creator. Because God is perfectly holy and just, there are consequences for doing wrong, and we must face judgment for our actions. Think about if someone in your family was horribly injured by a thief who entered your home. The thief was arrested and appeared in court before a judge. What would you think of the judge if he just released the thief and did not punish the crime? You would think he was a bad judge, right? A good and righteous judge delivers consequences for sin. God must do the same.

And while you may think you are basically a good person, I am guessing that all your thoughts haven't always been perfect, kind, good, and holy. We have a problem because of our sin. The Bible says that all have fallen short of the glory of God (Romans 3:23) and that the wages of sin is death (Romans 6:23). Because of our sin against a holy God, we deserve death and an eternity separated from Him.

Now, you may be thinking right now that no one can be perfect. And you are correct! None of us are righteous enough to earn our way into Heaven. Therefore, we are without any possible hope if left to our own devices. But that is where God, in His love for us, stepped in to provide a solution.

John 3:16-17 tells us, "For God so loved the world that he gave his one and only Son, that whoever believes in him shall not perish but have eternal life. For God did not send his Son into the world to condemn the world, but to save the world through him."

God sent Jesus to pay the price of our sin. Jesus lived a perfect life. He was without sin and therefore, was a worthy party to make payment. But the payment was something so horrible, that many times people have a hard time believing that someone would do this for them. Jesus allowed Himself to be crucified on a cross, facing an excruciating death, and in doing so, He took the punishment that should have been ours. Death. Our sin was paid for by the blood of Jesus.

But equally amazing is that Jesus didn't stay dead. On the third day after His crucifixion, He rose from the dead. And the evidence for the actual and physical resurrection of Christ is astounding. (Take a look at the *Case for Christ* by Lee Strobel).[84] The Son of God rose from the dead and was seen by over 500 witnesses, in 12 different locations, over 40 days.

You see, Christians believe not only that Jesus died in their place and paid the penalty of their sin, but they also believe that He rose from the dead and that they will spend all of eternity with Him. That is the future for which Christians rely upon, based on the authority of God's Word.

Though where we spend all of eternity following our earthly existence is paramount, the start of your relationship with God begins here on earth. Becoming a Christian means recognizing that you are in need of a Savior. It means not only believing and confessing that Jesus is your Savior, that He saved you from the penalty of sin (an eternity away from Him), but also submitting to Him as Lord of your life. There is a surrender that takes place. And while that may sound like a lot to swallow, keep in mind you are yielding your life to the One who set aside His glory to come to earth, to die in your place. He sacrificed Himself freely for you because He loves you! Isn't that amazing? The Creator of the whole world loves YOU!

And there is nothing you can do to earn that love. Jesus' sacrificial death on the cross is a free gift. We stand innocent before the Righteous Judge not because of what we have done, but because of what His Son did for us. We are found "not guilty" because of the blood Jesus shed on our behalf.

Scripture tells us that once we believe in Jesus, His Holy Spirit comes and dwells within us. He is alive in us. Sure we will still sin, but as we learn and grow, our desire is to be more like Jesus. And once you have entered into this relationship with God, you are His child. "Yet to all who did receive him, to those who believed in his name, he gave the right to become children of God" (John 1:12). As His child, you have full access to Him, and He delights in you.

If you are feeling the need for a Savior, if you want to receive Jesus into your life, tell Him now. And once you do that, I encourage you to tell someone else. Tell a friend. Tell your pastor. If you are not in a Bible-teaching, Bible-believing church, find one. It is of great importance to be connected to a local body of believers. They will help you grow, and they will challenge, encourage, and equip you. Meanwhile, I am so glad you are in this study. There may be many new concepts and ideas, but hang in there. Following Jesus will be the absolute best adventure of your life!

LEADER'S GUIDE

Thank you for leading a group through this Bible Study! I am praying for you. Below you will find a brief plan for each week. Use it exactly or switch it up to meet the needs of your group.

Introduction Week

Welcome your group: If you have women who do not know each other, be sure to allow time for introductions and sharing. Go around the room and ask the women to share something about themselves. Name tags are very helpful for the first few weeks!

Share prayer requests and open in prayer: Provide time each week for ladies to share prayer requests, and then lift the requests up to the Lord. Remind the group of the need for confidentiality on things that should not be shared beyond the group. Depending on the size of your group, decide if you will go around and offer for the ladies to pray if they would like, or if you and/or another will alone pray for requests.

Distribute workbooks.

Watch Introduction Video: All videos can be accessed at KristenTiber.com/GreaterGloryVideos. An email address is required to view the lessons. Video lengths are listed on the video library page. All videos <u>except</u> the introduction video have an accompanying study guide to be filled out in the workbook.

Worship: If possible, spend time together in worship. Song suggestions are listed on the same webpage as the videos.

Close in prayer.

All Other Weeks

Share prayer requests and open in prayer.

Discussion: Discuss answers from the workbook indicated by ✢. Allow for any other thoughts and comments about what was studied this week. *See bonus discussion questions for Week Three below.

Watch the online video.

Week One: *Show Me Your Glory*

Week Two: *Birthing an Ichabod*

Week Three: *Scattered Seed*

Week Four: *Fuel for the Fire*

Week Five: *Present Sufferings*

Worship. Song suggestions are listed on the same webpage as the videos.

Close in prayer.

*Bonus Group Discussion Questions for Week Three:

> ✢ To which of James' examples of patience can you most relate or learn from in the current season you are in?

> ✢ What are some characteristics of God on which we can rely when we find ourselves needing to be patient?

Acknowledgements

Thank you to all the wonderful ladies at my church who participated in this Bible study as I taught the material in person and who encouraged me to put it into print. As always, it is a privilege to do life together—to love, laugh, and sometimes cry our way to living lives that bring Him greater glory.

Thank you to my very special beta Bible study group (Megan, Amy, Susan, Jess, Susie, Meg, Tina, Jody, Deanna, and Loretta) who diligently worked through the study workbook over five weeks, meeting together at my house and on zoom when necessary. I greatly appreciate your valuable feedback, dedication, and encouragement. I knew you were supportive, but I was completely blown away by your kindness, generosity, and care not only for me, but also for one another. Our time together is something I will always treasure.

Special thanks to Tara, the friend and editor who causes me to grapple and sweat, but in the end makes my writing stronger. I am so very thankful for you. You're the best!

Many thanks to the Christian Creative Mastermind group not only for your friendship, but also for your help, support, and brainstorming sessions. I may not stay up as late as you all, but the retreat was wonderful and I look forward to more!

To Melinda Martin of Martin Publishing Services: you were amazing to work with. I felt at ease knowing my cover and manuscript were in your capable hands. Your standard for quality, keen eye for design, and attention to detail raise the bar for independent publishers again and again. Not to mention, I so loved hearing your Texan accent on the videos you made for me.

To Holly Michelson of Five Five Media Co.: I am so thankful the Lord paired us together for this film project. You were such fun to work with and an inspiration as a Christian business owner. I pray for great blessings on your business and family.

Thank you also to these individuals who helped in a variety of ways: Hannah, Jess (Jessie Anne Photography) and Pastor Jack. Your guidance, support and help were such blessings to me.

And as always, many thanks to my wonderful husband Dan, my two kids Peter and Anna, and my mom for reading, listening, supporting, and encouraging me to pursue that to which God has called me. You are the greatest of my blessings!

Works Cited

1 Professor Thomas A. Rohm, "What Exactly is 'Glory'?" Barabbas Road Church, www.barabbas.com/glory [accessed 12/18/2019].

2 Paul David Tripp, "The Doctrine of Glory." Date of Publication: August 20, 2018. https://www.paultripp.com/articles/posts/the-doctrine-of-glory-article [accessed 12/16/2019].

3 Ibid.

4 Ibid.

5 Ibid.

6 Madeline Kalu, "What is the Meaning of Shekinah Glory." www.Christianity.com/wiki/christian-terms/what-is-the-meaning-of-shekinah-glory.html [accessed 12/18/2019].

7 *Strong's Exhaustive Concordance*, [online], https://biblehub.com/hebrew/3519.htm [accessed 09/29/2020].

8 Professor Thomas A. Rohm, "Glory to God in the Highest—Part 1." Barabbas Road Church, http://www.barabbas.com/glory-to-god-in-the-highest-part-i/ [accessed 09/29/2020].

9 Walter C. Kaiser Jr., *Hard Sayings of the Bible.* (Downers Grove, Illinois: InterVarsity Press, 1996) 155.

10 Rohm, www.barabbas.com/glory [accessed 12/18/2019].

11 Michael W. Anderson LP & Timothy D. Johanson MD, *The Gist: The Essence of Raising Life-Ready Kids.* (Carol Stream, Illinois: Focus on the Family, 2019).

12 "Bible Timeline." https://biblehub.com/timeline/ [accessed 9/19/2020].

13 Kalu, www.Christianity.com/wiki/christian-terms/what-is-the-meaning-of-shekinah-glory.html [accessed 09/29/2020].

14 John Piper, *God's Passion For His Glory.* (Wheaton: Crossway Books, 1998) 37.

15 Kaiser, 155.

16 Chip Ingram, "Good to Great in God's Eyes - Pursue Great People, Part 2." [podcast] *Living On The Edge*. https://livingontheedge.org [accessed 12/24/2019].

17 Chip Ingram, *Why I Believe* [Study Guide]. (USA: Living on the Edge, 2019) 31.

18 Warren W. Wiersbe, *The Bible Exposition Commentary: History.* (Colorado Springs: Victor, an imprint of Cook Communications Ministries, 2003) 218.

19 Charles Haddon Spurgeon, *The Treasury of the Bible*, Vol 1. (Grand Rapids: Baker Book House, 1981) 632-633.

20 Jerry Bridges, "Jesus Challenges the Pharisees." https://www.ligonier.org/learn/articles/jesus-challenges-pharisees/ [accessed 1/05/2020].

21 Rabbi Ted Falcon PhD & David Blatner, *Judaism for Dummies*, 2nd ed. (New Jersey: John Wiley & Sons, Inc., 2019) 241.

22 *NIV Biblical Theology Study Bible*. (Grand Rapids: Zondervan, 2018) 450.

23 *Strong's Concordance*, [online], https://biblehub.com/greek/5088.htm [accessed 9/30/2020].

24 *Strong's Exhaustive Concordance*, [online], https://biblehub.com/greek/5088.htm [accessed 9/30/2020].

25 *Strong's Concordance*, [online], https://biblehub.com/greek/616.htm [accessed 9/30/2020].

26 Wiersbe, 218.

27 *NIV Biblical Theology Study Bible*, 451.

28 Ibid.

29 Bruce Wilkinson & Kenneth Boa, *Talk Thru The New Testament*, Vol. 2. (Nashville: Thomas Nelson Publishers, 1981) 468.

30 Warren W. Wiersbe, *The Bible Exposition Commentary: New Testament*, Vol. 2. (Colorado Springs: Victor, an imprint of Cook Communications Ministries, 2001) 378.

31 Paul David Tripp, "The Problem with Patience." [audio], https://www.sermonaudio.com/sermoninfo.asp?SID=56081035174 [accessed 1/10/2020].

32 Ibid.

33 *Strong's Exhaustive Concordance*, [online], https://biblehub.com/greek/3114.htm [accessed 9/30/2020].

34 *Thayer's Greek Lexicon*, [online], https://biblehub.com/greek/3114.htm [accessed 9/30/2020].

35 *Life Application Study Bible: King James Version*. (Wheaton, Illinois: Tyndale House Publishers, Inc., 1989).

36 *Amplified Bible*, [online], (La Habra, California: The Lockman Foundation, 2015). https://www.biblegateway.com/passage/?search=James%205:7-9&version=AMP [accessed 10/1/2020].

37 Wilkinson, 465.

38 Bruce Wilkinson & Kenneth Boa, *Talk Thru The Old Testament*, Vol.1. (Nashville: Thomas Nelson Publishers, 1983) 197-198.

39 Wiersbe, *The Bible Exposition Commentary: New Testament*. 379.

40 Ibid.

41 "Patience." Lexico, [online], https://www.lexico.com/en/definition/patience [accessed 10/1/2020].

42 *Strong's Concordance*, [online], https://biblehub.com/greek/5278.htm [accessed 10/1/2020].

43 Wiersbe, *The Bible Exposition Commentary: New Testament*. 336.

44 Jon Bloom, "Lord, Align My Heart With Yours." *Desiring God* https://www.desiringgod.org/articles/lord-align-my-heart-with-yours [accessed 1/27/2020].

45 Ibid.

46 *NIV Biblical Theology Study Bible*, 1967.

47 Ibid, 1968.

48 Ibid, 1968.

49 Ibid, 1967.

50 Catherine Marshall, *A Man Called Peter: The Story of Peter Marshall*. (New York: McGraw-Hill Book Company, Inc., 1951) 61.

51 "End-A-Rooney." *Liv and Maddie*. written by Danielle Hoover and David Monahan, directed by Andy Fickman, Disney, 2017.

52 Bruce H. Wilkinson & Larry Libby, *Talk Thru Bible Personalities*. (USA: Walk Thru Bible Ministries, 1983) 37.

53 Scripture quotation taken from the New American Standard Bible® (NASB), Copyright © 1960, 1962, 1963, 1968, 1971, 1972, 1973, 1975, 1977, 1995 by The Lockman Foundation. Used by permission. www.Lockman.org

54 "Renown." Dictionary.com, [online], https://www.dictionary.com/browse/renown?s=t [accessed 7/21/2020].

55 J. Vernon McGee, *Thru the Bible*, Vol 2. (Nashville: Thomas Nelson Publishers, 1982) 157-158.

56 Scripture quotation is from The ESV® Bible (The Holy Bible, English Standard Version®), copyright © 2001 by Crossway, a publishing ministry of Good News Publishers. Used by permission. All rights reserved.

57 Beth Moore, "Names of God: The Lord of Hosts." [podcast] Living Proof Ministries. (Beth is quoting from the Lexical Aids of the Old Testament.) https://subsplash.com/livingproofwithbethmoore/messages/mi/+ytmn3cr [accessed 9/2/2020].

58 *The Holy Bible, English Standard Version*. [online], (Wheaton, Illinois: Crossway Bibles, 2001). https://www.biblegateway.com/passage/?search=1%20Samuel%2017%3A45&version=ESV [accessed 10/3/2020].

59 Elisabeth Elliot, *Suffering is Never for Nothing*. [audiobook], (Nashville: B&H Books, 2019).

60 John 1:28 and John 10:40.

61 Wiersbe, *The Bible Exposition Commentary: New Testament.* 334.

62 McGee, 438.

63 Wiersbe, *The Bible Exposition Commentary: New Testament.* 335.

64 McGee, 441.

65 *NIV Biblical Theology Study Bible*, 1905.

66 Marvin R. Vincent, D.D., *Vincent's Word Studies in the New Testament*, Vol 2. (Peabody, Massachusetts: Hendrikson Publishers, 1985) 202.

67 Beth Moore, "Ephesians: Armed for War." [podcast], Living Proof Ministries. [accessed through the LPM app].

68 *Life Application Study Bible: King James Version.*

69 *Strong's Concordance*, [online], https://biblehub.com/greek/1320.htm [accessed 10/6/20].

70 HELPS Word-studies, [online], https://biblehub.com/greek/1320.htm [accessed 10/6/20].

71 Wiersbe, *The Bible Exposition Commentary: New Testament.* 337.

72 Ibid, 337.

73 Vincent, 206.

74 McGee, 441.

75 Beth Moore, *Daniel.* (Nashville: LifeWay Press, 2006) 46.

76 Ibid.

77 Ibid.

78 Ibid.

79 Piper, 45.

80 Piper, 46.

81 Elliott, [audiobook].

82 *Amplified Bible*, [online].

83 Paul David Tripp, "The Doctrine of Glory." [online].

84 Lee Strobel, *The Case for Christ,* Updated & Expanded Edition. (Grand Rapids: Zondervan, 2016).

Made in the USA
Monee, IL
17 May 2021

68802817R00085